D1585424

THE GREEK
VEGETARIAN

ALSO BY DIANE KOCHILAS

The Food and Wine of Greece

THE GREEK VEGETARIAN

More than 100 recipes inspired by the
traditional dishes and flavors of Greece

Diane Kochilas

PHOTOGRAPHS BY CONSTANTINE PITTAS
ART BY VASSILIS STENOS

ST. MARTIN'S PRESS ❧ *New York*

THE GREEK VEGETARIAN. Copyright © 1996 by Diane Kochilas. Photographs copyright © 1996 by Constantine Pittas. Illustrations copyright © 1996 by Vassilis Stenos. All rights reserved. Printed in the United States of America. No part of this book may be used or reproduced in any manner whatsoever without written permission except in the case of brief quotations embodied in critical articles or reviews. For information, address St. Martin's Press, 175 Fifth Avenue, New York, N.Y. 10010.

Production Editor: David Stanford Burr
Book design by Gretchen Achilles
Map of Greece by Martie Holmer

Library of Congress Cataloging-in-Publications data

Kochilas, Diane.
    The Greek vegetarian: more than 100 recipes inspired by the traditional dishes and flavors of Greece/Diane Kochilas; photographs by Constantine Pittas; illustrations by Vassilis Stenos.
        p. cm.
Includes bibliographical references and index.
ISBN 0-312-14608-6
1. Vegetarian cookery.   2. Cookery, Greek.   I. Title.
TX837.K63   1996
641.5'636'09495 — dc20   96-20453
                                                                                                          CIP

First St. Martin's Press edition: November 1996
10 9 8 7 6 5 4 3 2 1

FOR KYVELI, WHO WAKES UP AND SAYS
"MOMMY, I WANT TO COOK."

CONTENTS

ACKNOWLEDGMENTS

Many people help to bring a book into the world. This one wouldn't exist if it weren't for my editor, Barbara Anderson, an avowed vegetarian, who loved the idea from the start and whose queries and pencil made everything within these pages work better. I am indebted, too, to Marian Lizzi, whose involvement at the end ensured that everything ran smoothly. I'd like to thank my agent, Doe Coover, whose melifluous voice over so many long and distant phone calls always calms me down, and Nancy Jenkins, who generously led me to Doe. Special thanks and a prayer go to the late Diane Cleaver, my agent at the time this book was conceived.

I'd like also to thank Constantine Pittas for his relentless deliberation over every photograph. I am indebted to Roxanni Matsa, whose wines inspired us during the long photo sessions and who graciously gave us her estate in Kanza to shoot the cover photograph. Thanks, too, to Gretchen Achilles for her inspired design.

Much appreciation goes to my friend Katerina Gounaraki, who turned her cordon bleu attentions to the recipes and helped to make them as sound and savory as possible. I owe much, too, to Eric Moscahlaidis, friend and in many ways savior.

Many cooks around Greece shared their recipes with me. Some, such as Chris Veneris, Xrysanthos Karamolengos, and Dimitri Bliziotis, are pros; most though are simple home cooks who opened their kitchens and homes with warming hospitality and with what the Greeks call, untranslatably, *filotimo*.

Last, but never least, I must thank my family: my sister Athena, for letting me take over her New York kitchen for one entire summer to test many of the recipes herein; her boys—Thomas, George, Paul—and my mother, Zoe, for tasting, criticizing, and (usually) devouring the results; and Connie and Trif and Kris and Katherine for their love.

My best critic and best friend is the man I've shared table and life with for the last fifteen years. Vassilis shows me Greece anew every day. His painting of the landscape we both love so much opens each main section—subtly, persistently, gracefully, perceptively, like him.

INTRODUCTION

A few years ago, a small book, called *The National Bean Soup* was published by a famous Greek folklorist, Ilias Petropoulos. In this book, the author pleads for the return or at least the resuscitation, of the cooking of our grandparents' generation. The national bean soup was his leitmotif for the very soul and identity of the Greek table. Like the country's flag, the simple bean soup is a dish that crosses all socioeconomic lines. It is something every Greek grew up on, identifies with, and still savors. Bean soup mirrors the simplicity—and terse elegance—of our cooking, and reflects its regional differences and seasonality. It is the consummate vegetarian meal, and the consummate Mediterranean meal, as well—combined with hearty bread, dressed with raw olive oil, washed down with wine.

Greek cooking, with few exceptions, has always sprung from the garden. In ancient Greece, there existed an entire school of ascetic vegetarianism, established by the mathematician and philosopher Pythagoras, who forbade his disciples to eat meat and who lived a long and energetic life on a diet of honey, barley, millet, and raw or boiled vegetables. Even for non-Pythagoreans, though, the daily diet of the ancient Greeks was based on legumes and grains, especially barley—foods that have sustained Greeks through the long trials of history and remain staples to this day.

The barley breads of the ancients, for example, are not dissimilar to today's quite common Cretan barley rusks. In other parts of the country there are wheat-based porridges, eaten in celebration of certain saint's days, that hearken to the gruels of our ancestors. A primitive soup made with the Mediterranean trinity of bread, wine, and olive oil is still the harvest meal in many parts of the country. Goat's milk and cheese are also as basic to our diet today as they were twenty-five hundred years ago. Olives, wild greens, figs and other fruit, as well as garlic, onions, leeks, raisins, capers, nuts, and herbs, still compose the list of ingredients that are woven inextricably into our culinary lore.

Greek cooking boasts myriad recipes for vegetables, legumes, greens, and grains in endless combinations that call for little embellishment beyond olive oil, salt, and the refreshing, enhancing juice of the lemon. Meat has never played a primary role, in part because it has always been expensive in Greece. But even today, when meat is no longer considered a luxury, it often plays a subordinate role, combined (in small portions) with greens or beans or other vegetables—in dishes that are essentially vegetable stews enriched with a little lamb or pork or beef. The backbone of the cuisine has always been what is harvested, in either wild or cultivated form, from the earth.

All over Greece, the ties to the land manifest themselves in customs as old as day. The Greek landscape is at once brutal and sweet, bright with a merciless yet nourishing sun, and relentlessly dry. The land has never yielded its bounty easily in Greece; there is always a struggle, and with it an ensuing humility and inherent reverence. How else to explain the touching folk customs that still endure in rural areas? In Ithaca, for example, villagers so treasure that most significant of Mediterranean foods, the olive, that they give names to their olive trees as though the trees were human.

On any given day in the Greek countryside, people forage casually for wild greens to be used in a salad or a pie, and on any given day in the farmer's markets that travel to every neighborhood in every city, the importance of vegetables in the daily diet is palpable. In the cities of Greece, something like 80 percent of the population shops in farmer's markets, not supermarkets, for their vegetables and fruits. Even the name for these road-show emporiums is apt: *laïkea agorá*, or "people's markets." "Everything that's in season can be had at these markets: chestnuts, cabbage, pomegranates, quince, turnips, and spinach in winter; artichokes, tender broad beans, and fresh garlic and onions in spring; then, finally, the profusion of vegetables that marks the summer and early fall. The old women who go home with a shopping cart full of cabbages to put up in brine, or with bags spilling forth luscious red peppers to roast and preserve in olive oil, evince a tie to the earth that even today seems innate.

Cooks still go to great lengths to secure the vegetables or herbs or greens that come from a particular place—their place. I have a friend who sends me box loads of wild mushrooms that he forages himself from Mount Pelion, and when I go to the bus station to pick up the packages I always see other people doing exactly the same thing. One woman waits for a box of *furtkia*, a small apple also native to Mount Pelion. At another time of year, the cargo changes to *fteria*—fiddlehead ferns—and to *tsitsiravla*, the pickled blossoms of wild pistachios. Another friend's mother sends packages filled with seasonal greens from her village in Crete—things as obscure now as borage or fresh chick-peas. The Greek table is a cornucopia of both seasonal and regional produce. I once heard a delicious dish of stuffed eggplants described as "having the whole garden inside." It is an observation that could apply to the entire Greek vegetarian tradition.

To my mind (and palate) some of the most beautiful Greek dishes are the ones that proved to be too obscure to include here, dishes that nowadays only subsistence farmers could possibly make because the ingredients required are so inextricably tied to the seasons and to an agrarian way of life. In Crete, for example, there is a delicious dish that calls for young almonds. It is difficult to describe the taste of fresh, immature nuts. Almonds, when they are still in their green, soft skins, are both sweet and laced with the most delicate hint of bitterness, and they are moist, as though sprinkled with dew. The old Cretan recipe calls for cooking them lightly with olive oil, salt, onions, fresh tomato, and, at the end, lemon juice. How can one reproduce a dish like that in a New York kitchen, or like the *aïkomatiba* of Corfu, another luscious dish also bound indelibly to one season, the fall? It is made by slightly drying young figs, chopping them and kneading them with ouzo and pepper, shaping them into large thick disks, and wrapping them in chestnut leaves to dry. I have included one old agrarian recipe in these pages, for a dish I have named simply Harvest. It comes from Crete, and it literally combines all the nuts and vegetables of autumn: pumpkin, chestnuts, red peppers, leeks, and olives.

The Greek vegetarian table honors regional distinctions, geography, historical influences, and the ingenuity of the home cook when faced with limited ingredients. With so little to work with, Greek cooks have had to come up with new ways to cook the same basic ingredients. In Santorini, for example, where the humble split pea and a particular indigenous tomato are the larder's traditional staples, there must be twenty different ways to cook split peas—from soups to baked terrines to fava, a kind of creamy puree. Other ingredients follow a regional path around the country. Winter squash, for example, is usually baked into sweet pies in the northwest of Greece, into a savory baked casserole with walnuts and garlic in Macedonia, into patties fragrant with mint in the Peloponnisos, and into savory pies and stews and pilafs in the eastern Aegean.

One of the main influences in the evolution of the vegetarian table, and one that can't be easily overlooked, is the role of religion. Until very recently, most Greeks adhered to the fasting calendar of the Greek Orthodox Church, so for forty-eight days before Easter, forty days before Christmas, and for lesser fasting periods throughout the year they abstained completely from meat and animal products (certain fish are allowed). On the highest holy days, such as Good Friday, even olive oil was forbidden. Such a regimen meant that for just about half the year one went off meat, cheese, milk, yogurt, eggs, and butter. One of the unique aspects of Greek vegetable and grain cookery is that many dishes come in two versions—one for Lent and one for the rest of the time.

There is a whole school of dishes called *lathera*—oiled—that are essentially Lenten dishes but that are so inherently good they make for some of the best fare of the entire table. These include a bevy of fresh and dried bean stews; artichoke, potato, and pea or broad bean stew; delicious stewed eggplants or squash; and just about anything else that can be cooked in one pot, slowly, with an unabashed quantity of olive oil as the main flavoring agent. These dishes are meant to be main courses, another unique aspect of the vegetable cookery in Greece. Rarely are vegetables relegated to side-dish status. Most are meant as the day's main meal, to be accompanied by bread, wine, a few olives, and some fruit afterward.

In the last decade or so, Greeks have earned the dubious distinction of being Europe's greatest meat eaters, yet they continue to consume large quantities of the old foods, too—greens, infinite vegetables, fruits, and, of course, bread. They haven't replaced the foods that have sustained them for eons with the foods of affluence; instead, they have just made the plate big enough to fit both. Greeks today are, in a sense, accidental vegetarians, but the traditions of vegetable cookery go back too far to forfeit easily. The soul of the whole cuisine is still in the foods with which we have a direct connection—in the dishes that come to table just picked from the garden or hillside.

This book is an attempt to show the breadth and wealth of both traditional and newer Greek vegetable and grain dishes. There is, I think, a good mix of classics, a few obscure agrarian dishes that seem oddly fitting for our tastes today, and a number of recipes, such as the vegetarian *souvlaki*, that are inspired by Greek flavors and traditions. There is, too, a good mix of nondairy recipes and of dishes for the less austere vegetarian that include cheese, eggs, and milk. My own feeling is that one should be able to eat everything in moderation, that "nothing in excess" is the best advice for enjoying and savoring good food.

THE GREEK VEGETARIAN PANTRY

There is a certain elemental quality to all the cooking of Greece that separates it from the cooking to the east and to the west, that is, from the cooking of Turkey on one side and of Italy on the other. It is a quality that goes beyond the mere simplicity of preparations. It is as though an underlying sensibility guides the best Greek cooks to leave well enough alone, to keep the bounty of the earth as close to its original form as possible. Produce tastes different here, better, authentic, full of the original glory nature intended. The raw ingredients taste so good on their own in Greece that there is little need to alter them with complicated recipes or to camouflage them with sauces. It is difficult, though, to reproduce the flavors of the Greek garden without actually being near one. I encountered this difficulty time and again, especially when trying to replicate dishes in my city kitchen that I had first tasted in the countryside. One can't. Trying to is quixotic. So, the advice that every cook gives time and again to anyone with a recipe book in hand is to seek out the best produce, the freshest raw ingredients, and the ones that come to market from as close to their source as possible. Beyond that, the Greek vegetarian table is dependent on a few essential ingredients. These are the staples without which the vegetarian larder would be bare. First among them is the olive and its oil, bread, then cheese, yogurt, nuts, and herbs.

OLIVES AND OLIVE OIL

For a few days one recent October, I went down to the Mani to taste olive oil. The region, the easternmost peninsula of the Peloponnisos, is so dry and barren that the landscape seems lunar. But from Mani's naked earth comes liquid gold—the fruitiest, most delicious olive oil I have ever tasted. We drove deep into the region, to a village called Riglia about 40 kilometers (24 miles) south of Kalamata, to see a small stone press. It was early in the season, but in Mani the harvest starts a few weeks, sometimes a full month, before that of the rest of the Peloponnisos. When we arrived, the press was churning. Young green olives poured from a conveyor belt into a kind of masher, which turned them, rather unceremoniously, into a dark sludge. Then, in an enormous round tub, that pulp was crushed into oil under the weight and rotation of two huge stone wheels. Out gushed the raw green oil, *agourelaio* (meaning "unripe" in Greek), streaming forth regally from an unadorned spigot. It was warm. I had never seen that before, and had never tasted warm oil. We ran pieces of toasted peasant bread under the faucet to catch some of the oil, sprinkled each piece with sea salt, and enjoyed one of the best meals of our lives. I knew then, really for the first time, how old, primal, essential is olive oil to this part of the world.

Greece is the world's third largest producer, but first in the production of extra-virgin oil. Of the thirty thousand tons total that it produces yearly, 75 percent is extra-virgin. Sadly, more than half of Greece's olive oil is sold in bulk to Spain and Italy. It's an interesting business, to say the least, and one worth mentioning, even if briefly, here. Agents for the Spanish and Italian importers swarm to Laconia and Messinia (Kalamata) in the middle of winter, well after the harvest has begun, and when prices stabilize. The big deals—a thousand tons, say—are always kept quite secret, but the day the shipment goes out, the size of the sale is on egregious display. An oil tanker (outfitted specifically for edible oils) waits in the port of Kalamata. On the dock and leading up to the ship is a chain of oil trucks, each waiting its turn to pump Kalamata's gold into the enormous ship. Messinia is first among Greek olive-oil producing prefectures, so the winter is a busy time here. Nevertheless, there is still ample oil left for Greeks to enjoy in great quantities. On average, the per capita consumption of olive oil in Greece is the highest in the world—about twenty quarts per year.

Olive oil is made from many different varieties of olives—none the same as those cured for use as table olives. The ancient Greeks thought the best oil came from the slightly unripe olive—like the *agourelaio* of Mani. There is a world of difference in the oil from region to region. The areas around Kalamata produce some of the best, from the small *coroneiki* olive. The oil of Mani is exceptionally fruity and peppery, and next (in my opinion) are the oils from Coroni and then from Petrina in Laconia. One will find such place-specific oils only at the source itself. But it doesn't matter. All the extra-virgin oil from the southern Peloponnisos promises to be luscious and fruity. Crete is also a great producer of olive oils, and from the western part of the island also comes some of the best in Greece (on equal footing, to my palate, with Mani's oil, but milder, and more "buttery.") After the Peloponnisos and Crete, Lesvos, then Corfu, have the highest concentration of olive trees.

Every village in Greece, though, usually has an olive press, and during the harvest families wait their turn to bring their olives to the cooperatives to be pressed. Their payment for the use of the press is in oil. It is a system that keeps many families supplied with their own oil, from their own trees, year-round. So tied are Greeks to the harvest that even today Greece is the only country in the European Community where civil servants are given special leave each fall to go and tend to their olives. I was surprised to learn that not every variety of oil olives, regardless of the care with which they are handled, can produce extra-virgin olive oil. In some islands of the eastern Aegean, for example, the oil is notably more acidic. It doesn't matter; every Greek believes the oil from his own backyard is far superior to olive oil from anywhere else.

In *Prospero's Cell*, Lawrence Durrell writes that "the whole Mediterranean seems to rise out of the sour, pungent taste of black olives between the teeth. A taste older than wine, a taste as old as cold water." I felt his words come alive for me that fall day when we visited the old press in Mani. Nothing is more basic to the Greek table than the olive and its oil.

THE TWO BASIC OLIVE-OIL DRESSINGS
Olive oil combined with lemon juice and herbs (*latholemono*) or with vinegar (*lathoxido*) are the two simplest and most familiar tastes on the Greek table. With equal frequency, both sauces are used over salads of raw or boiled vegetables.

LATHOLEMONO (olive oil and lemon juice)

2 parts extra-virgin olive oil

1 part fresh strained lemon juice

Salt and freshly ground black pepper to taste

Herbs (optional), such as oregano, thyme, savory, marjoram, snipped fresh dill, or chopped fresh parsley

Whisk together the olive oil and lemon juice, add the salt, pepper, and herbs, and continue whisking for a few seconds more to combine. Or shake all ingredients together in a small jar. Pour immediately over salad.

LATHOXIDO (olive oil and vinegar)

2 parts extra-virgin olive oil

1 part red wine vinegar

Salt and freshly ground black pepper to taste

Herbs (optional), such as oregano, thyme, savory, marjoram, snipped fresh dill, or chopped fresh parsley

Shake all the ingredients together in a small jar and serve immediately.

A PRACTICAL GUIDE TO GREEK OLIVES

For all its ubiquity, the olive is also the source of much confusion. Most consumers recognize Greek table olives by their place names (Kalamata, Atalanti, Amfissa, for example), by the curing process they undergo (cracked), split, cured in salt, in vinegar brine, or salt brine, or olive oil), or simply by their colors (black or green). It seems as though there are dozens of "different" varieties, when in fact there are only three main scientific varieties and several secondary ones that are commercially important. They just happen to come in many sizes, and from many different parts of Greece, so that they all look different.

All olives change from green to black as they mature, and all are bitter and inedible unless cured. Depending on the variety and the curing method, some olives are processed unripe, or green, while others are left to mature and darken on the tree. Others still are purposely harvested late, when their skins are leathery and wrinkled.

The most common and quickest way to cure olives is to soak them for several days in a lye solution and then to season them accordingly. This process yields the worst-tasting olives. Some olives are cured in a vinegar brine, others in a salt brine. There is a dry-cured process, too, in which olives are packed in salt and left for several months. Wrinkled black olives have generally been dry-cured.

BUYING GREEK TABLE OLIVES

The three most important varieties of Greek table olives are the *kalamata*, the *conservolia*, and the *halkidiki*. Of secondary importance are the *megaritiki* and the *thrubolea*. None is called by its scientific name at the supermarket, however. Following is a look at each and the common names they go by:

Kalamata These shiny, brownish-black, tight-skinned olives with an almond shape are the best known Greek olives outside Greece. Surprisingly, they rank third in commercial importance inside Greece. The name is confusing, since "kalamata" in this case refers to both the name of the variety and the name of the city in the Peloponnisos where this olive is most common. Adding to the confusion is the fact that "kalamata" olives are also cultivated widely in Samos and Crete. The kalamata is the most highly prized black olive, and is usually slit (*harakti*) on two sides and preserved in vinegar and/or olive oil.

Conservolia Recognizable at markets under the names volos, amphissa, agrinio, stylida, and atalanti, this large, oval olive accounts for more than 80 percent of all the table olive production in Greece. It starts off a rich dark green when unripe and changes into a whole spectrum of different colors as it matures: greenish-yellow, greenish-red, mahogany, and, finally, dark bluish-black. Conservolia is the most versatile Greek olive, processed with equal success as both a green and black olive. When harvested green, the conservolia can be stuffed, cured in salt brines of varying strength, and finally turned into what the Greeks call *tsakistes*, or "cracked" greens. Harvested black and mature, it is cured in a vinegar brine, or as a black "slit" olive.

Halkidiki These are large olives, usually harvested green, that come from the region of the same name just east of Salonika in northern Greece. Halkidiki olives are characterized by their firm, meaty pulp. They range in color from green to amber and chestnut, and they are usually cured in a salt brine.

Megaritiki Colloquially called *tsakistes*, or "cracked," this variety grows mainly in Attica and almost always is cured as a green olive. Megaritiki olives are easy to recognize. They are the small and medium-sized green olives with the pointy "nipple" on one end and are most often found flavored with lemon and garlic.

Thrubolea or *Throumba* These are the wrinkled, reddish-brown, mealy olives that are indigenous to the eastern Aegean islands and to the Cyclades. They are left to ripen on the tree and are salt-cured. A similar variety, which is pitch black and pleasantly oily, also grows on Thásos (the Thásos throumba).

CURING OLIVES

From the end of October in Greece one can find hard, green, uncured olives at the farmer's markets. In the United States, Greek greengrocers often sell uncured California olives in the fall, too. It is not difficult to cure olives at home.

GREEN OLIVES IN SALT BRINE

Take 5 pounds of fresh green olives, thoroughly washed, and place them in a large basin with enough water to cover. Place a plate and weight on top to keep the olives submerged. Let the olives steep for 5 to 10 days, changing the water every day. Taste the olive—it is ready to be placed in brine when it is no longer exceedingly bitter. Measure out the water and prepare a salt brine by mixing enough coarse salt with the water so that when a raw egg submerged in the water floats to the top (an area of about one inch in diameter will break the surface of the water). Approximate quantities are 3 1/2 ounces salt to 1 pint water. Place the olives in the brine. Squeeze 5 to 6 lemons as well as some bitter (Seville) oranges, if they are available and add the juice to the olives. Season the olives with whole twigs of dried thyme, marjoram, oregano, or wild fennel. Olives processed this way will take abut 6 months to cure.

GREEN OLIVES IN BITTER ORANGE JUICE

This is one of the masterpieces of the Greek peasant kitchen. Take cured green olives (above), slit them on two sides with a razor or sharp paring knife, and place them in a bottle. Cover them with fresh strained bitter orange juice and pour about 1 inch of olive oil on top. The olives will keep this way for months, and the fragrant juice of the bitter oranges will permeate them subtly. This is a spe-cialty of Crete and Rhodes.

THE GLORIOUS CHEESES THAT ARE GREEK

When most Americans think of Greek cheese, they think of feta, which is, in fact, the fastest growing cheese in terms of consumption in the United States. But there is more to Greek cheese than that. In the last few years, Greek cheeses have moved beyond the ethnic market: Many stores that carry a variety of foods from around the world now offer Greek regional cheeses, including feta from several different places as well as other, artisanal cheeses.

The art of making cheese is as old as the tale of Ulysses, who walked in on the cheese-making Cyclops in Homer's epic to find him nestling his small, fresh, white goat's milk cheese. The industry, though, is young but vibrant. Greeks eat an inordinate amount of cheese — about forty pounds a year, each. Roughly 70 percent of the estimated one million tons of sheep's and goat's milk produced annually is used to make cheese, as is about 30 percent of the 700,000 tons of cow's milk. Greek cow's milk cheeses are generally not available in the United States because of importation quotas. Brine-cured cheeses — essentially feta — account for more than two thirds of 190,000 tons of sheep's and goat's milk cheese produced in Greece each year.

Several things distinguish Greek cheeses from those made in other parts of Europe. In Greece, the majority are made from either sheep's or goat's milk. More than any other single factor, the country's many wild grasses and greens put their mark on the flavor and texture of Greek cheeses. Sheep and goats graze freely, and are nourished on the likes of chervil, clover, sorrel, and dandelion. Cheesemaking moves with the seasons, with most cheese at least commercially, produced from November to May, after the animals have given birth and nursed and when the terrain is lush with flora from the winter rains. Following is a brief list with descriptions of Greek cheeses both popular and obscure.

BRINE CHEESES

Feta First among the brine cheeses, the most popular and famous Greek cheese, and the fastest-growing cheese in America. Like roquefort, camembert, edam, and other cheeses whose origins and production are place-specific, feta is traditionally Greek. Brine cheeses long have been made throughout the Balkans, and in recent years northern European countries started producing white brine cow's-milk cheeses that have little to do with the traditional product. But recent changes in European law have made it illegal for other countries to use the name "feta," after the year 2002.

Feta is a soft, white, sharp cheese made almost exclusively from sheep's milk, and sometimes from a combination of sheep's milk and up to 30 percent goat's milk. By law, Greek feta is *never* made with cow's milk. The cheese is aged for a minimum of two months, either in barrels or in tins. The former is losing ground to the more convenient, easier-to-ship tins, but feta produced in the Peloponnisos is usually barrel-aged, while that produced in the north of Greece is usually aged in tins. Although feta is made in many parts of the country, it generally is not produced in the islands except for Cephalonia; it is the traditional shepherd's cheese of the mountainous mainland. The region of Arcadia in the Peloponnisos and Epirus in northwestern Greece are the most famous feta-producing regions in the country.

Teleme Another brine cheese, similar to feta but made with a combination of sheep's, goat's, and cow's milk and always aged in tins. Telemes is the traditional cheese of northeastern Greece, especially Thrace and Drama.

Sfela This is a sharp brine-aged cheese made in the southern Peloponnisos. Its name comes from the Greek *sfelia*, which means slice. Sfela is much harder than feta or telemes, and tends to be saltier. Sometimes it is called locally "feta of fire" because the curd, once cut, is scalded. Traditionally it is made from unpasteurized sheep's milk or from a mixture of unpasteurized sheep's and goat's milk. It is an excellent grating cheese.

Batsos Anyone visiting the wine-producing region of Náoussa is sure to run into batsos at one of the local tavernas. Batsos is a semihard white brine cheese made from sheep's or goat's milk and that used to be a by-product of another cheese, manouri. It is low in fat and has a sour, sharp taste. Unlike feta, telemes or sfela, batsos is filled with air pockets.

SOFT WHITE CHEESES

Touloumotiri Visitors to Samos and Mitilini (Lesvos) are likely to find cheesemongers in both the main towns and villages selling touloumotiri. Its name literally means "skin cheese." Traditionally this soft, peppery cheese is aged for several months in goatskins. It is a specialty of the eastern Aegean islands, and cheesemongers there still sell it directly from the skin. A slightly shocking sight, but the cheese, soft, white and very pungent, is unforgettable.

Galotiri Another very unusual and very sharp soft white cheese. Its consistency is like ricotta with cream added to it, and its name literally means "milk cheese." Although produced in small quantities all over Greece, and most often for personal consumption, its production is strictly seasonal. The cheese is made from ewe's milk in July and August. It is eaten as a table cheese, almost as a spread like American cream cheese, but is also a favorite in summer salads (replacing the ubiquitous feta) and in savory pies. It is usually sold from very small barrels at the cheese counters of major supermarkets in Greece. You can also make it at home by combining yogurt and feta (see recipe, page 17).

Kopanisti The name means "pounded" and refers to two different cheeses. The first, a soft, traditional, sharp, and extremely pungent cheese, is produced in the Cycladic and eastern Aegean islands. Especially well known is the salmon-colored kopanisti from Mykonos. Traditional kopanisti is left to ferment for several months, often in skins, during which a roquefort-like bacteria develops, giving the cheese its hue and piquancy. Depending on where the cheese is from, it is either pinkish or blue in color. It is delicious and strong, but not for the faint of heart. Secondly, kopanisti refers to the whipped, peppery cheese dip made with feta, olive oil, a little lemon juice, and sometimes herbs (see page 31).

SEMIHARD CHEESES

Kasseri After feta, probably the best-known Greek cheese. Kasseri is a yellow, spun-curd cheese made from either ewe's or cow's milk. It is mild and resembles the Italian provolone in consistency. It is generally eaten as a table cheese. Kasseri should be pliable and resilient, but solid. Avoid kasseri whose interior is pocked with tiny holes.

Graviera An aromatic, flavorful yellow cheese with a hard rind made either from sheep's milk or from cow's milk, depending on the region. Graviera is sweet, mellow, and nutty—one of the most delicious Greek cheeses. The sheep's milk gravieras come from Crete, Lesvos, Dodoni, Arta, and Kalpaki. (Crete is actually the most famous graviera-producing region, and here one of the unusual ways to serve the cheese is with honey and walnuts.) Cow's milk graviera, which is yellower and a little creamier, is made mostly in Tinos, Syros, Naxos, Corfu, Larissa, and Serres.

HARD CHEESES

Kefalotiri A very hard, light-yellow sheep's or goat's milk cheese with a sharp tangy flavor. It is made mainly in Crete, as well as in Naxos, Cephalonia, Thessaly, and Epirus. It is a popular grating cheese.

Kefalograviera Another pale-yellow cheese with a hard rind and an abundance of small air holes. As its name indicates, in both flavor and texture it falls somewhere between graviera and kefalotiri. It can range from sweet and mild to quite piquant. Kefalograviera is the cheese of choice for grilling and frying, but it can also be eaten as a table cheese.

Ladotiri Another unusual cheese, whose name means "oil cheese." Traditionally, the cheese, which is shaped like miniature barrels, was steeped in olive oil and aged for several months. Two islands in Greece are known for their ladotiri: Lesvos and Zákinthos. On Lesvos it is extremely difficult to find authentic ladotiri nowadays. Commercial producers dip the cheese in paraffin instead of olive oil. On Zákinthos, though, a bevy of artisanal cheesemakers have kept up traditions, and the local ladotiri is pungent and delicious. It can be found easily in the farmer's cooperative market in the island's capital.

Formaella This is a sharp, cylindrical cheese made in the foothills and mountain villages of Parnassus, especially in Arahova. It is made mainly with sheep's milk and was traditionally eaten as a grating cheese.

Metsovone This is a rich, hard, smoked yellow cheese made in Metsovon, hence its name. It resembles smoked provolone. Metsovone is made in large sausagelike loaves, usually from raw cow's milk. It is equally delicious as a table cheese or fried (*saganáki*), as the local tavernas serve it.

San Mihali One of the few traditional exclusively cow's milk cheeses made in Greece. San Mihali is a specialty of the island of Syros (it is named for the Roman Catholic church on the island). It is hard and piquant and was traditionally eaten locally as a grating cheese.

WHEY CHEESES

These account for a surprisingly large part of total cheesemaking in Greece. Most whey cheeses are made from the residual liquids of feta. The cheeses are seasonal, usually produced from December to June, because at that time of year local greens and other flora are most plentiful and milk is the creamiest.

Mizithra The word dates to the sixteenth century, when it referred to a kneaded cheese. Mizithra is a feta by-product. Traditionally, the whey from feta is combined with some whole milk. The curds are heated, collected, drained, and lightly salted. Mizithra is sold either as a soft table cheese or aged into rock-hard balls and used as a grating cheese.

Anthótiro The word literally means "blossom cheese," after the way the curds rise to the tops of the vats and open in a shape resembling blooms. The cheese is similar to ricotta, but lightly salted. It is eaten fresh with jam or honey, and often baked into sweet pastries, especially around Easter.

Manoúri This is a creamy, buttery mild white cheese that is sold in log-shaped loaves. It is excellent as a desert cheese, topped with honey or with poached fruits, and complements the sweet wines of Greece exceptionally well.

OTHER REGIONAL CHEESES

Included here are the cheeses a lucky and curious traveler is likely to encounter in various parts of Greece.

Pretza A soft, creamy, very sharp and pungent white cheese made in Zákinthos in the spring. Imagine a fiery cream cheese. Locals spread it on bread and drizzle olive oil over it for breakfast.

Kraáotiri or *Ghilómeno* These are two similar sheep's milk cheeses sure to win an oenophile's heart, since they are aged in the lees (dregs) of the local wine. These wine cheeses are found exclusively in certain Greek islands. Kos and Nyssiros, for example, are known for the log-shaped wine cheese called krassotiri. In Sifnos, we found the ghilomeno, after the local word for lees. Ghilomeno is shaped into small barrels and aged for several months in thick wine residue until what results is an extremely powerful hard cheese. Traditionally, the cheese was aged in pits, filled with must or lees, and covered. Nowadays, you are more likely to find it submerged in small plastic barrels.

Petrotiri A sheep's milk cheese that comes from the mountain villages on the islands of Tinos and Andros, and literally means "rock cheese," after the way it is made. Once coagulated the cheese is pressed between small flat rocks. It has a lovely pungent rind and a creamy interior. It is certainly one of the most beautiful cheeses in Greece.

Kathoura This mozzarella-like goat's milk cheese made on the island of Ikaria is shaped into fist-sized balls and either served fresh or aged in brine.

Megithra A specialty of the Cycladic islands, and one of the few Greek cheeses that has anything added to the curds. When the curds are first cut, either oregano or thyme is mixed in. The cheese is then placed in goatskins for several months to mature.

Chloro The fresh white goat's milk cheese from Santorini and other Cycladic islands, and the main ingredient in the island's well-known Easter sweets, the *melitinia*.

Greek Chèvre There are two producers in Greece who make cheese under the name "chèvre." The largest is the Averoff Dairy in Métsovon, which produces a chèvre nothing like the traditional French cheese. Averoff's rendition is aged, pungent, and extremely hard. It is delicious, but it's not anywhere near authentic. An artisanal cheesemaker who runs a farm on the island of Evia, however, has managed to produce several chèvres of distinction. His name is Lazaros Maltezos, his dairy is in the town of Stira, and his soft goat's milk cheeses are available widely in the better markets around Athens.

BREAD

Although I haven't included many bread recipes in this book, it would be impossible to consider the vegetarian traditions of the Greek table without giving bread its due. Together with olive oil, bread is the basis of everything Greeks eat. Meals are simply not enjoyed without it, and in times of hunger it was often the only thing Greek peasants had to eat. There are many old recipes for whole dishes based on bread. In Rhodes, for example, one dish is touchingly called crumbs and oil—*ladopsibia*—and is a deliciously simple combination of onions and old bread cut into cubes and cooked in olive oil with tomato, salt, and pepper.

Another old Rhodian dish was a kind of bread soup—stale bread poached in saltwater and served sprinkled with sheep's milk cheese and olive oil. Another bread soup hearkens back to the earliest days of the Mediterranean. Called *zoupa* and still savored during the arduous season of the olive harvest in Cephalonia, it is a heartwarming broth made with toasted bread over which is poured warm wine and olive oil. Dishes as simple as these appear in regional cooking all over Greece.

Bread is also a fundamental ingredient in dips and spreads, in patties, and sometimes in stuffed dishes. *Skordalia*, the well-known garlic-powered dipping sauce, uses bread (or potato) as its base.

In ancient Greece, the most prized bread was made from wheat, although it was expensive. Barley was a commoner and cheaper grain, and the stuff of peasant gruels, but loaves were made from wheat, which was usually emmer, a hard red wheat. White and brown bread were both familiar, as were both unleavened and leavened breads. Baking powder and wine yeast were used as leavening agents. There were oven-baked breads, crock-baked breads, breads baked under ashes, drop scones, and pancakes. Porridge and gruel, made from barley and from combinations of barley and emmer wheat were both common on the daily menu of the ancients. (Today, barley is still widely consumed in Greece, not in the form of gruel, but in the form of rusks. The closest thing to porridge today are the many countryside soups thickened with *trahana*, a hard, pebble-sized homemade pasta.)

Despite the seemingly great variety of breads and wheat dishes, the best breads in the ancient world were considered the whitest, or *polytelus*, which means luxury, a belief that took millennia to dispel. Until the early 1980s, when the bread industry was finally deregulated, most Greeks still wanted the fluffy, white, nutritionally barren luxury loaves. The nutrient-rich whole-wheat and multigrain breads that one finds nowadays in almost every bakery in Greece are newcomers.

There were a number of interesting dishes made from wheat, and others made from pastry, most notably *plakounta*, something that sounds like a precursor to pizza. It was essentially a flat grilled piece of dough topped with whatever was available—cheese, onions, honey, or fish.

Bread was highly ritualistic in the ancient world and still is today. Demeter, goddess of the earth, the family, the hearth, was honored once a year with breads in every shape and form. As the myth goes, Demeter's daughter Persephone was stolen away to Hades, the Underworld. To avenge her loss, Demeter made the earth barren. Zeus granted her release, but Persephone erred by eating in Hades, which obliged her to spend a portion of the year there. The myth of course fables the cycle of nature, of planting and harvesting, winter and spring. Each year before the harvest, a procession of Athenians of every social and economic class set out for Eleusis to honor her, bearing their bread tokens—sculpted loaves said to look like ploughs, animals, or other symbolic shapes relating to agriculture, all offerings of thanks and hope for a fruitful year.

Until the 1950s and 1960s, ritualistic breads were still very much a part of Greek folkways. Many of the regional bread customs have died in the last few decades, but others are still very much intact.

Each Christmas, for example, Greeks still make a special bread called *christopsomo*, which is studded with dried fruits and nuts, symbols of fertility and abundance. In the Mani and other parts of the Peloponnisos, traditionally on Christmas Eve, you can still find the *lalangia*, fried strips of dough dipped in honey and nuts that were believed to ward off unwanted spirits.

At New Years, Greeks cut the *vassilopita*, a bread that always has a coin inserted into it for good luck. But this tradition changes dramatically from place to place. Among Greeks from Poli and from other places in Asia Minor, the *vassilopita* is always sweet, rich with eggs, and yeasty. It is usually flavored with orange rind, with lemon, and with spices such as mahlepi and mastic. In some parts of Greece, *vassilopita* is simply a dense cake. In Epirus, it is a savory pie. The coin is ubiquitous, and whoever gets the piece with the coin will have a lucky year.

Lent in Greece begins with bread, this time an unleavened oval-shaped loaf called *lagana*. On the island of Amorgos at the start of Lent, the custom is to make small anthropomorphic sculpted breads for children called *lazaroi*. Traditional, too, in many parts of Greece is the *kyria sarakosti*, a flat inedible bread sculpture shaped like a woman with six feet, each one in correlation to the six weeks of the fast, and broken off one by one until Easter finally arrives.

At Easter, Greeks eat *tsoureki*. This is another egg-laden and yeasty loaf that is studded with red-dyed eggs and is usually braided. The *kouknoukas* of Kassos is another Easter bread, usually shaped like a snake or like a human figure, and always decorated with a red-dyed egg. In Santorini and other Cycladic islands, one specialty of the Easter table is a hard thick rusk flavored with saffron and anise. In June, on the island of Sifnos, around the feast day of the Holy Spirit in early June, bread shaped like doves is made by bakers all around the island.

Bread in the everyday life of the Greeks can be just as unusual as ritualistic loaves made around certain holidays. There are many different kinds of daily bread in Greece, but among the most extraordinary are the chick-pea bread called *eptazymo*, found in Crete and in parts of Macedonia; the dried, ring-shaped barley rusk that is one of the hallmarks of the Cretan kitchen; and finally the corn breads, some sweet, some savory, found all over the north of the country.

Paximathia, or rusks, made from either chick-pea, whole-wheat, or barley flour, are another of the unusual breads of Greece. Rusks are still made and eaten widely all over the country, and have always been the bread that farmers took with them as a snack in the fields. Like so much of the food in Greece, rusks are yet another mirror of the economy of the Greek home cook. Housewives used to bake—in their own outdoor ovens most of the time—about once every ten days. They would make several days' worth of fresh bread and then, with the ovens turned off but still hot (cavernous, wood-burning ovens retain their heat much longer than our gas or electric ovens do), they would cut several loaves into thick slices and dry rather than bake them in the warm oven. Making *paximathia* was nothing more than a way to preserve bread. The thick dried slices are drizzled with a little water and olive oil, which softens them, and eaten in lieu of a fresh loaf, or in salads, with tomatoes, olives, and feta. In Crete, one kind of *paximathi* is the *kouloura*, a beauti-ful, dark, ring-shaped dried bread that is drizzled with olive oil and served topped with grated tomato and aromatic oregano. It is a dish so simple, so healthful, and so exquisitely elegant.

YOGURT

Every day at 5:30 A.M. outside my husband's studio in an old part of Athens, a man in his late sixties drives by on a three-wheel pickup, megaphone in hand, hawking his "traditional" homemade yogurt, which is made from 100 percent unpasteurized sheep's milk. He is one of the few old-timers left in the city who still do this—most have gone the way of the milkman in America. But yogurt is still made by dozens of small artisans all over the country, includ-ing Athens. On every container the name and phone number of the manufacturer appears, and there seems to be one in every neighborhood. Yogurt has been fundamental to the Greek diet for a very long time.

Greeks mostly eat sheep's and cow's milk yogurt, although one can find goat's milk yogurt in rural areas. They also eat strained yogurt, which is thick and creamy, with a tex-ture akin to that of sour cream (see instructions below).

In cooking, yogurt is used mainly as a medium for dips and spreads. *Tzatziki*, the cucumber and garlic salad, is probably the best-known yogurt-based dish in the Greek kitchen, but there are also tangy salads made with carrots and yogurt, roasted eggplant and yogurt, beets and yogurt, and one unusual recipe found in both Cretan and the Politiki cooking for purslane and yogurt. In the cooking of the Pontian Greeks (who have lived on both sides of the Black Sea for centuries), yogurt is sometimes used as a poaching liquid for eggs. Eggs cooked in yogurt or served with yogurt also appear in Epirus. Greeks also use yogurt, together with a lot of eggs, as a filling for a savory pie, called *yiaourtopita*. There are many recipes for vegetables, most notably spinach or eggplant, baked with yogurt, as well as pasta dishes with yogurt and garlic from all over the country. Greeks also make a cheese with yogurt and feta, called *galotiri*, in which the feta is combined with yogurt and left to stand for a few days (see recipe on page 17). The result is a very creamy, tangy soft cheese that is used as a spread or table cheese.

I borrow here from Paula Wolfert's encyclopedic book *The Cooking of the Eastern Mediterranean* to explain how to make strained yogurt at home.

DRAINING YOGURT

Yogurt, whether homemade or all-natural low-fat commercial, consists of a delicate balance between curds and whey. Yogurt thins out when vigorously stirred, breaks down when heated without a stabilizer, and "weeps" when salty foods are added. I always drain low-fat yogurt to obtain a thicker consistency: Place lightly salted yogurt in a sieve lined with cheesecloth and let it drip for 30 minutes to 24 hours. (You can substitute nonfat yogurt but the resulting texture is a little chalky.)

Within an hour from the time you begin, your yogurt will lose about 20 percent of its liquid, acquiring the consistency of light whipped cream. This is about right for use in salads. Within several hours, your yogurt will lose almost half its volume and acquire the consistency of sour cream. In this form it is perfect for dips, sauces, and soups, for thickening vegetable purees, and as an accompaniment to rice and bulgur pilafs and stuffed vegetables.

Whenever you are draining yogurt, save the whey for cooking vegetables or for using as a drink. It's reputed to be good for the kidneys.

Drained yogurt, lightly salted, keeps longer in the refrigerator than commercial or homemade yogurt. Cover and store in glass or plastic containers and keep refrigerated for up to two weeks.

Goat's milk yogurt has a tangier flavor than cow's milk yogurt. You can use it drained for dips and salads.

Sheep's milk yogurt, which is naturally rich and dense, needs less draining for dips and salads.

GALOTIRI

2 1/4 pounds Greek feta

6 cups drained yogurt

1 cup milk

Salt to taste

1. Crumble the feta by hand until it has the consistency of cottage cheese. Place in a large bowl and mix thoroughly with the drained yogurt and the milk. Taste it and adjust seasoning with more salt if desired.

2. Cover the mixture and place in the refrigerator. Mix it twice a day and leave it, covered, in the refrigerator for 1 week. By the end of 7 days, the *galotiri* will be pleasantly tangy and creamy.

BEANS

Beans and legumes are among the most basic foods on the traditional Greek table, whether that table is strictly vegetarian or not. The broad bean, the chick-pea, and the lentil have been eaten since time immemorial. Greeks eat many other kinds of fresh and dried beans, too.

In spring, the first beans that come to market are fresh broad beans, which are almost always eaten unshelled when very tender in stews and omelets. In late spring a host of fresh beans, including string beans, butter beans, runner beans, fresh black-eyed peas, flageolets, and cranberry beans—all of which are usually shelled and often frozen for use in hearty winter stews—make their appearance at the farmer's market. Most fresh beans in the Greek kitchen are cooked as *latbera*—over low heat for a long time with tomatoes, potatoes, and a lot of olive oil. Fresh black-eyed peas, called *ambelofasoula* in Greek, make for a delicious salad, with a little garlic and some fresh herbs.

Dried beans are relished with equal enthusiasm. The most unique dried beans are the *gigantes*, or giant beans, which resemble lima beans but are bigger. These are baked with tomatoes and other vegetables into luscious casseroles, and are sometimes simply boiled with a little olive oil, lemon juice, and oregano. Other, smaller white beans are cooked into stews and the national bean soup, which is a mélange of navy or cannelloni beans, tomatoes, celery, onion, and often hot pepper. Chick-peas, like lentils and broad beans, have one of the longest histories in the Greek kitchen. They are cooked with greens or with eggplant into rich casseroles, boiled for salad with rice or bulgur, and made into a very simple but delicious soup that is the national dish of Sifnos, an island that is part of the Cyclades. Dried black-eyed peas, one of my own favorites, are often dispelled by Greeks, since the humble black-eyed pea sustained them through years of hunger during World War II. Lentils are also common in the Greek kitchen and are used in soups and pilafs.

ONIONS

Probably the single most important flavor in the vegetarian pot is that of the humble onion. I can recall a conversation I had with a woman from Poli (Istanbul) about the classic meatless stuffed grape leaves called *dolmades yialantzi* (see page 145). She quizzed me on whether I knew the secret of the simple rice and herb stuffing. "Onions," I answered. "Six, maybe eight." "Your numbers are off," she scolded. "Try twenty, and you'll succeed in making the dish properly."

Unlike elsewhere in the Mediterranean, Greek cooks continue the ancient practice of using the onion more as a seasoning than as a vegetable in its own right. Few are the dishes where the onion shines first. Yet the humblest member of the lily family (asparagus and tulips and the yucca are also part of the same plant tribe) melds into the backdrop of countless Greek dishes. The onion has been forever present in our stews and stuffed dishes and is eaten with equal enthusiasm raw, in salads and as a garnish over bean soups and sauces.

purees. Other members of the onion family, including the leek, the spring onion, and the scallion, are also important in the vegetarian diet, but don't play nearly so important a role. Greek cooks use several different kinds of dried onions. Red onions are more prevalent than white, although there is a large, flat white onion, called *belousiotika,* after the town in Zákinthos to which it is native, that is very similar in taste to the sweet vidalia. There are large *nerokremmyda,* water onions, which are like what we know in the U.S. as the yellow Spanish onion. Another important dried onion is the small stewing onion, which is used whole.

The onion has been a staple in ancient Greece since at least 500 B.C., and Attica was famed for its onion fields. It was always held to possess both medicinal and invigorating properties: In the Iliad, we hear of strong sweet Pramnian wine being served with a scraping of goat's cheese and onion on top. Olympic athletes were said to have to consume an onion the size of a fist on the morning before the games, and one the size of a thumb at night to help them sleep.

GARLIC

One of my favorite places in all of Athens is a small basement warehouse on the edge of the Central Market where what seems like the whole country's supply of garlic is cleaned and distributed. At any time of the day, several old women sit on the floor surrounded by mountains of garlic, which they are busy either braiding or tying into clusters. On the streets around the market and at the farmer's markets, garlic is often sold by the Gypsies.

One never quite thinks of garlic as having a season, but in Greece the plant's cycle is evident at market. In spring, right around the start of Lent, tender stalks of fresh garlic arrive. These are eaten raw (usually with *taramosalata,* the carp roe and bread dip). In summer, dried garlic is tender, with a pearly white, translucent skin. By the end of winter, when the supply is nearing its bottom, garlic is wrinkled and brittle.

Like its Allium-family cousin the onion, garlic is indispensable to Greek cooking, often dominating the flavor of certain dishes. Garlic is used in stews and myriad other savory dishes, but it also plays first fiddle in dipping sauces such as *skordalia,* and in yogurt-based salads such as *tzatziki.* Greeks love the satisfying taste of garlic and nuts, and there are several sauces that call for walnuts and garlic or almonds and garlic.

NUTS

There is not a specific word in Greek for the generic term, "nut." In the culinary logic of the Greek cook, nuts fall under the general umbrella of dried fruits, *xirous karpous.* Nonetheless, they are very basic to our diet, eaten readily as snacks, but also important in cooked dishes, stuffings, and sauces (as well as in sweets). The two most significant nuts in the Greek pantry are the walnut and the almond. Pine nuts appear mostly in stuffings, and filberts and pistachios are usually eaten as a snack, although the latter is an important component in several pastries and spoon sweets. For the vegetarian, nuts have always provided a substantial source of protein.

ALMONDS

When my daughter was just two, she learned to say "aman," her version of almonds, and she loved them fresh off the tree in our yard. For one whole summer she forced me, the way only a two-year-old can, to sit for hours on end cracking open the velvet green shells. It gave her a good laugh, and it gave her a good source of nutrition in the unsettling days of vacation. Almonds are a lot better than chips, after all, for a child too distracted by goats and birds and the sea and all the other wonders of the countryside to pay much attention to meals. I let her do what man has done naturally for millennia—feed off nuts, the ultimate convenience food.

Nuts in general have been seminal to the Greek pantry for thousands of years, and almonds are among the most revered. Botanically, the almond is *Prunus amygdalus*, and it is really the kernel of a fruit related to the peach and to the plum. Like most of what belongs to our (by now) native table, the almond traveled from the East to the West, and began its journey long before anyone was interested enough to record it. Some sources point to western India as its native land, others trace its ancestry to Asia Minor or to Babylon. It has been unearthed in the Neolithic levels under the Palace of Knossos in Crete, and in the Bronze Age storerooms under Aghia Triada, also in Crete. The Greeks were the first Europeans to cultivate it, and, according to Athenaeus, the famed chronicler of the food of the ancient world, Naxos was celebrated for its almonds.

In modern Greek cooking, the almond (blanched) is sometimes used as a base for *skordalia*, and as a thickener in an interesting tomato sauce in which eggplants are cooked, and as a little gem to slip into eggplants before they are pickled. A fabulous dish from Crete calls for immature almonds sautéed with tomatoes, but where to find such treasures in the urban kitchen?

WALNUTS

Walnuts, the leitmotif in Greek pastry making—*baklava, karydopita* (walnut cake), *thiples* (fritters sprinkled with walnuts and honey), and *melomacarona* (walnut-stuffed, syrup-soaked Christmas cookies)—are also an important addition to the savory cuisine of the Greeks. Walnuts, even more than almonds, are used ground as a thickener and base for many sauces. In Macedonia, ground walnuts add body and a pleasant, earthy, and discreet bitterness to *melitzanosalata* (eggplant salad) and to *skordalia*. Walnuts and garlic combine in another interesting dish from the north, as a sauce over baked eggplant or pumpkin. One of the most unusual dishes is for a walnut-studded miniature omelet from the rural traditions of Crete. The ancient Greeks used to crush walnuts for their oil, a delicacy that unfortunately has been lost to modern Greeks, who no longer do this.

HERBS, SPICES, AND THE FLAVOR COMBINATIONS

One of the oddities of Greek cooking is that tradition prefers dried herbs over fresh, and that the vast majority of herbs are used less for their aromatic value in the kitchen and more for their medicinal value in the form of infusions and tisanes. Sage, for example, readily used elsewhere in the Mediterranean, is almost unheard of in the Greek larder. But sage tea is one of the most popular warm drinks.

Only parsley, wild fennel, and dill are used almost exclusively fresh. Mint is used both fresh and dried, but oregano, thyme, savory, marjoram, bay leaf, rosemary, and the myriad other herbs that lace the Greek countryside are almost always dried before they make their way into the pot. Basil is generally not used in cooking at all, although from the start of the summer until the Day of the Holy Cross on September 14, when it is brought to church, pots of it sit outside almost every household, for its aroma is said to ward off evil spirits (and mosquitoes).

As for spices, Greeks make generous use of cinnamon, cloves, and allspice in sauces and other savory dishes. Rarer are spices such as mastic, the crystal resin from a tree in the pistachio family indigenous to Chios, and that is used in some breads, in some unusual sauces, and then relatively commonly in sweets. Cumin is common in the cooking of northern regions. Fennel seeds, sesame seeds, and mahlepi (the inner seed of a type of cherry) are used sporadically in bread baking, pastry making, and some savory dishes.

GREEK FLAVORS

What is it that makes a dish Greek, or for that matter French, Egyptian, Italian, or anything else? Every cuisine is, of course, the ever-changing sum of countless influences, both historical and geographical. But from the point of view of the humble cook I think there are certain defining flavors, or combinations of flavors, that make a dish unquestionably Greek. I remember once, a few years ago, a dish of roasted beets with allspice, prepared by my colleague Rosemary Barron at a dinner at the James Beard Foundation in New York City. I had never seen such a recipe in any of my travels across Greece seeking out traditional dishes. But when I closed my eyes and tasted what she had made, it was as though I could taste the Greek landscape. She had managed to trap it, if even ephemerally, in one quick bite of those beets. There are a host of spice and herb combinations that seem to me fundamentally Greek. Among them are the following:

- ◆ LEMON AND DILL

- ◆ LEMON AND OLIVE OIL

- ◆ LEMON, OLIVE OIL, OREGANO, AND GARLIC

- ◆ LEMON AND EGGS (*AVGOLEMONO*)

- ◆ TOMATOES AND CINNAMON (IN SAUCES)

- TOMATOES, HONEY, VINEGAR, AND DILL
- GARLIC GROUND WITH MINT (SOMETIMES WITH THE ADDITION OF WALNUTS)
- GARLIC AND VINEGAR
- ANISE (OR OUZO) AND PEPPER
- OLIVES, ORANGE, AND FENNEL

Although there are specific uses for each of these combinations in the repertoire of Greek cooking, they can make many different foods seem, at the least, Greek-inspired.

PICKLES

It used to be a standard household chore, from the summer to the early fall, to put up all sorts of vegetables in brine. Pickles, *toursia,* are still an important part of the larder, and one of the best *mezes* to serve with ouzo and tsipouro (grappa). But fewer and fewer women go to the bother of making stuffed baby eggplants preserved in vinegar, or pickled whole cabbage heads, or *volvous,* the bitter, pinkish bulb of the water hyacinth, which is a regular feature on the Lenten table. Nevertheless, it would be difficult to exclude pickled vegetables from the vegetarian pantry. In the countryside, people often make *toursia* from wild mushrooms, from hard-boiled eggs, from small hot peppers and roasted red peppers, from eggplants, artichokes, cauliflower, and just about anything else culled in excess from the garden.

PICKLED BRUSSELS SPROUTS WITH CELERY AND HOT PEPPER

Lahanakia Vryxelon Toursi

2 pounds brussels sprouts

1 cup chopped celery tops, leaves included

3 hot green or red peppers, seeded and cut into 1/4-inch rings

1 1/2 cups water

2 cups white wine vinegar

1 teaspoon salt

1/2 teaspoon sugar

1 teaspoon whole peppercorns

Olive oil

We tried this in a seaside tavern called Odyssea up the mainland coast of Greece. The cook-owner is a Greek who runs the place with his whole family and everything we ate except the fish was culled from their own garden. It was Lent, and we had asked for dishes that would be appropriate for us, since, for the first time, we had decided to fast the full forty days. Along with shellfish and squid and spinach-and-rice and cabbage salad came the following dish.

1. Wash and trim the brussels sprouts. Bring a large pot of lightly salted water to a boil and blanch the brussels sprouts for 3 minutes. Add the celery, bring back to a boil, and continue to blanch for another 2 to 3 minutes. Drain in a colander and rinse immediately with cold water. Place the vegetables in a 2-quart mason jar, together with the peppers.

2. Place the water, vinegar, salt, sugar, and peppercorns in a saucepan and bring to a boil. Pour into the jar over the vegetables. Let stand, uncovered, for 2 hours, or until cool. Pour in enough olive oil to cover 1 inch of the surface. Close the jar and refrigerate for at least 1 week before serving.

MEZE
GREECE'S LITTLE DISHES

MEZE: GREECE'S LITTLE DISHES

Just before finishing this book, I led a group of American journalists on a cook's tour of Crete, where one of our stops was the small village of Kalogerou, in the county of Rethymnon. We had gone to see a bread demonstration—in this part of the country every one of life's milestones is celebrated with handmade, highly ornate breads that are prepared by a kind of Kaffeeklatsch of village women. It was late when we arrived, and the street lamps were not working. The only source of light came from the fire under the local still. We entered the damp barn and found the father of the family we were to visit making the first of the winter's tsikoudia, the Cretan grappa. We drank some hot from the still and moved next door to the house, where, aside from the actual demonstration, we were greeted by a table full of food. "Just a little something to welcome you, some *mezethakia*," Argyro, our hostess, begged. There was Cretan graviera cheese (see page 11), olives cured in bitter orange juice, and bread; *skordalia*, peppers stewed in tomato sauce; and of course tsikoudia. This was Cretan hospitality in all its glory, and the *mezes* were the expression of that.

It is difficult to describe the sense of hospitality, or *filotimo*, that runs so deep among Greeks. It is a combination of earnestness, hospitality, openness, friendship, and sincerity. For a Greek, it is unthinkable to have a guest at home, if even for a little while, without offering him something to eat and drink. Even workers in the house—painters, plumbers, etc.—are fed a little something as the day wears on. *Mezes* are the little dishes that best fulfill the duty of the host—small offerings, small plates, that can be presented on a moment's notice. They might be nothing more than bread or olives or small portions of the day's main meal. There is also a whole host of dips and spreads, salads, and other quick food that count as *mezes* in Greece; they are the dishes by which people share a glass of wine or ouzo, or tsikoudia.

Mezes might be eaten as a kind of quick snack in the middle of the day, something you stop for between work and going home for the main meal; sometimes they are starters to a meal, and sometimes the meal itself. There are restaurants, called *mezethopoleia*, that serve nothing but small plates and they are the favored lunch and late-night spots of Greeks the country over. You pass by in the afternoon to share a glass with a friend or colleague, and end up nibbling on eggplant salad, fava, roasted peppers, fried vegetables with *skordalia*, and anything else that might be on the menu that day. There is a certain wisdom to eating this way—it is relaxing, casual, friendly—with the kind of food meant to be shared.

The dishes represented here are by no means the full repertoire of Greek vegetarian *meze*. There is really no such complete list; in fact, almost any dish in the book can be eaten as a *meze*. I have tried to keep the recipes as simple as possible. Stuffed vegetables and savory pies, even baked bean dishes, which are simple to prepare but require long cooking, are absent from the list. Instead, I've concentrated on the dipping sauces that Greeks love so much, on savory panfried dishes, and salads.

DIPS AND SPREADS

A WORD ON DIPPING SAUCES AND OTHER MEZES IN BOWLS

The term "dip" or "dipping sauce" is a bit of a misnomer when it comes to the Greek *meze* table, because there are many dishes that fall under those names that in Greece are considered salads. These include *tzatziki* and *melitzanosalata,* whipped cheese, and half a dozen other dishes. We might for practicality's sake consider them "dipping salads," since, in Greece, a snack or even an entire meal can be made up of almost anything plus bread.

Most of the following recipes are meant to accompany thick wedges of good bread, crudités, fried vegetables, even wild greens—so versatile are the dips and spreads of the Greek kitchen. They are all seasoned robustly. Greeks are not shy about using garlic or pepper or strong herbs such as mint.

Often, small bowls of two or three dips are put out at the same time. These are comfort foods you can turn to again and again, in between other dishes, for the length of the meal.

THREE CHEESE "SALADS"

Greek cooks make all sorts of spreadable "salads" with cheese, usually with feta. The two recipes below that include feta are both quite pungent. The third calls for one of my favorite Greek cheeses, manouri, which is a creamy whey cheese not unlike ricotta salata. The recipe included here is inspired by Dimitris Bliziotis, the very talented chef of Athens's largest catering house.

FETA CHEESE SPREAD
WITH MINT AND GARLIC

Skordalia me Feta kai Dyosmo

1/4 cup finely chopped fresh mint

2 to 3 garlic cloves, peeled and chopped

3 to 4 tablespoons extra-virgin olive oil, or more

1/2 teaspoon (or less) freshly ground black pepper

1/2 pound feta, rinsed and drained

1 to 2 tablespoons strained fresh lemon juice

Feta cheese whipped with garlic and mint is found both in the Ionian and in the north of Greece, in Macedonia. This is an unusual, pungent spread that makes a great dip with toasted bread or with crudités.

1. Puree the mint, garlic, olive oil, and pepper in a food processor until the mixture is like a paste, similar to pesto in texture.

2. Crumble the feta and add it to the processor. Pulse until smooth and creamy. Adjust seasoning with lemon juice and more olive oil if needed.

Yield: About 1 1/2 cups

THE GREEK VEGETARIAN

WHIPPED FETA

Kopanisti

1/2 pound feta, crumbled

Strained juice of 1/2 lemon (or more to taste)

3 to 4 tablespoons extra-virgin olive oil

1/2 teaspoon freshly ground black pepper (or more to taste)

The word for this spread, kopanisti, *literally means whipped or beaten. This is a classic taverna and buffet dish. I use it to dollop over pasta with fresh broad beans and tomatoes (see page 80).*

Place all ingredients in a food processor and pulse on and off for 2 to 4 minutes, until smooth and creamy.

Serve as a dip, with crudités or toasted bread wedges.

Yield: About 1 1/4 cups

DIMITRI BLIZIOTIS'S MANOURI AND GRAPE SALAD

Tirosalata me Manouri kai Stafilla

2 cups firm, sweet, seedless green grapes

1 pound soft Greek manouri or ricotta salata

1/3 to 1/2 cup milk, at room temperature

1 cup plain yogurt

4 tablespoons grated Cretan graviera cheese*

1 cup coarsely chopped walnuts

Dash of white pepper

Dimitri Bliziotis is a chef and caterer in Athens, and he served this "salad" at a dinner I was lucky enough to attend.

1. Wash the grapes thoroughly and set in a colander to drain completely. Wipe dry.

2. Combine the manouri, 1/4 cup of milk, and yogurt in a food processor and pulse on an off until creamy. Add the graviera and mix again. If the mixture is thick, add a little more milk. Keep refrigerated until ready to serve.

3. If the cheese mixture thickens too much and becomes unpleasantly pasty, just before serving adjust texture with additional milk. Toss in the grapes and walnuts. Season with pepper and serve, dolloped into radicchio leaves or in several small bowls garnished with mint.

Yield: 4 to 6 servings

*Graviera is available in Greek and Middle Eastern food shops as well as in international cheese emporiums. If unavailable, substitute gruyère or emmentaler.

THREE SALADS WITH YOGURT AND VEGETABLES

Yogurt is more a medium or base in the following recipes than an actual dressing. There are many recipes in Greek cooking for salads or dips in which yogurt—usually thick, tart, strained sheep's milk yogurt—is used as a main ingredient. They come from all over the country, as the following recipes attest.

BEET AND APPLE SALAD
WITH YOGURT DRESSING

Patzarosalata me Xinomilo kai Yiaourti

2 large beets, trimmed, washed, and peeled

1 large Granny Smith apple

1 to 2 garlic cloves, peeled and chopped

2 tablespoons capers, rinsed and drained

1/4 cup extra-virgin olive oil

1 1/2 cups drained Greek yogurt (see page 17)

Salt to taste

2 to 3 tablespoons red wine vinegar

This is a popular salad on the winter buffets of Greece, and one that seems to hail from Greece's Balkan neighbors.

1. Shred the beets. Peel, core, and shred the apple.

2. In a medium serving bowl, combine the beets with the apple, garlic, and capers. Add the olive oil and yogurt and toss to combine thoroughly. Season with salt and vinegar.

Variation: Replace the capers with 1/3 cup chopped walnuts.

Yield: 4 to 6 servings

CARROT TZATZIKI

Tzatziki me Karota

1 large thick carrot, or 2 medium ones, washed and peeled

2 cups drained yogurt (see page 17)

3 large garlic cloves, peeled and finely chopped

1 to 2 tablespoons chopped fresh mint leaves, or 1 teaspoon dried

Salt and freshly ground black pepper

3 tablespoons extra-virgin olive oil

2 to 3 teaspoons strained fresh lemon juice, or more to taste

Most people know tzatziki *as the garlicky cucumber-yogurt sauce that accompanies* souvlaki *or stands on its own in the standard repertory of* mezes. *Carrots with yogurt and garlic are a popular alternative among the Greeks of the East — the Pontians and Poli Greeks. I first tasted this at a taverna called Anatolia in a suburb of Athens, and subsequently had it several times in the tavernas around the city run by Asia Minor Greeks.*

1. Shred the carrots. (There should be about 1 cup, packed.)

2. Combine the drained yogurt, carrots, and remaining ingredients in a medium-sized bowl. Let stand for at least 1 hour before serving.

Variation: For cucumber *tzatziki,* substitute 1 large hothouse cucumber for the carrots. Peel it and shred it or cut it into small chunks. Drain it in a colander, then squeeze out the excess water between the palms of your hands. Combine with yogurt, garlic, mint, olive oil, salt, pepper, either lemon juice or vinegar, and, if desired, 2 teaspoons of chopped fresh dill.

Yield: About 3 1/2 cups

PURSLANE AND YOGURT SALAD

Glistrida me Yiaourti

1 pound purslane

1 1/2 cups drained Greek yogurt (see page 17)

1/3 cup extra-virgin olive oil

2 to 3 tablespoons chopped fresh dill

2 to 3 tablespoons red wine vinegar or strained fresh lemon juice

Salt to taste

Yield: 4 servings

I include this recipe here, immediately after the carrot tzatziki *as opposed to among the salads, because it seems more like a dip to me than a salad, and because it is very similar to* tzatziki. *Purslane and yogurt is a flavor combination found among the Greeks from Poli, today's Istanbul, as well as among home cooks on Crete. My belief is that the Asia Minor Greeks who settled en masse in Crete in 1922 are responsible for transplanting this recipe to the island. Purslane is a delicate green that is showing up in more and more green markets in the United States.*

1. Use only the leaves and tender shoots of the purslane. Wash and drain in a colander.

2. Combine the leaves and shoots in a bowl with the yogurt, olive oil, lemon juice, and salt. Mix well and serve either cold or at room temperature.

EGGPLANT PUREE WITH WALNUTS

Makedonitiki Melitzanosalata

2 large eggplants

2 to 4 garlic cloves, peeled and minced

1/2 cup shelled walnuts, coarsely chopped

1/2 cup extra-virgin olive oil

2 tablespoons strained fresh lemon juice

1 to 2 tablespoons red wine vinegar

Salt to taste

1/2 to 1 teaspoon sugar (optional)

1. Preheat oven to 450°F. Wash the eggplants and pat dry. Puncture the skin in several places with a fork. Place on an ungreased pan and bake for about 25 minutes, turning, until the skin is blistered and shriveled. Remove from oven and cool for a few minutes, until easy to handle.

2. While eggplants are roasting, pulse the garlic, walnuts, and 2 tablespoons of the olive oil together in a food processor until ground and pastelike.

3. Cut off the stem and cut the eggplant in half lengthwise. Using a spoon, scrape out the pulp, discarding as many of the seeds as possible. Add the eggplant, a little at a time, to the bowl of the food processor and pulse on and off. Add the lemon juice, vinegar, and remaining olive oil and pulse until well combined. The eggplant puree does not have to be perfectly smooth. Season with salt and add a bit of sugar if necessary, as eggplants sometimes impart a trace of bitterness.

Yield: About 1 1/2 cups

FAVA WITH SUN-DRIED TOMATOES AND CAPERS

Fava me Liasti Tomata kai Kapari

1/2 cup plus 2 tablespoons olive oil

1 medium red onion, finely chopped

1 cup yellow split peas, rinsed and drained

5 to 7 cups water

Salt

3/4 cup sun-dried tomatoes

3 scallions, trimmed and cut into thin rounds

1 large garlic clove, peeled and chopped

3 tablespoons capers, rinsed and drained

3 to 4 tablespoons sherry or balsamic vinegar

Yield: 6 servings

My friend Kosta, who manages a Greek food exporting company, keeps me supplied with sun-dried tomatoes, which he produces in the middle of the country, in Larissa. In agrarian Greece, sun-dried tomatoes used to be quite common, and still are a standard preparation at the end of each summer on the island of Chios and in parts of the Peloponnisos. The idea for this dish came from the way yellow split-pea puree—what the Greeks confusingly call fava *—is served in Santorini, where one local dish calls for topping it with stewed capers.*

1. Heat 1/3 cup olive oil in a medium-sized casserole or stewing pot. Add the onion and cook until soft, 6 to 8 minutes. Add the yellow split peas and toss to coat with the oil. Stir for 1 to 2 minutes. Add enough water to cover split peas by 2 inches. Cover and bring to a boil over medium heat. Reduce heat, uncover, and cook over very low heat, stirring occasionally with a wire whisk, to keep from sticking, for 1 1/2 to 2 hours, until the split peas are completely disintegrated. During the course of cooking, add water. When the split peas have reached the consistency of loose mashed potatoes, remove from heat and add salt to taste. Cover with a cloth and let sit for 1 hour. The mixture will bind considerably.

2. As soon as you begin cooking the split peas, place the dried tomatoes in a bowl with ample warm water and let them sit for 30 minutes, to rehydrate. Drain, but set aside 1/3 cup of the liquid. Chop the dried tomatoes.

3. Heat 2 tablespoons olive oil in a medium-sized skillet. Add the scallions and garlic and cook until soft. Add the dried tomatoes, capers, and tomato liquid, and stir for a few minutes until liquid has evaporated and tomatoes are soft. Remove from heat and set aside until ready to use.

4. Just before serving, pour in the remaining olive oil, save for 1 tablespoon. Adjust the salt and stir in the sherry or vinegar. Spread the split peas evenly onto a serving platter, top with the sun-dried tomato and caper mixture, and drizzle remaining olive oil over the top. Serve warm or at room temperature.

Note: You can replace the sun-dried tomatoes with 1 cup chopped plum tomatoes (canned are fine).

CREAMY EGGPLANT SALAD, CONSTANTINOPLE STYLE

Politiki Melitzanosalata

2 large, heavy eggplants (about 2 1/2 pounds total)

2/3 cup extra-virgin olive oil

Salt to taste

Pinch of sugar

3 to 4 tablespoons strained fresh lemon juice

Yield: 2 1/2 to 3 cups

The trick to this version of melitzanosalata *is to keep the eggplant as white as possible, which is accomplished by submerging the hot pulp in olive oil. I once watched Soula Bozi, author of several books on the Greeks of Constantinople, shamelessly pour two entire cups of oil into a bowl, later to be absorbed by the charred smoky eggplants. This is a toned-down version, but one that calls for ample olive oil nonetheless. As for the eggplants, look for firm, large, heavy ones, preferably with stout irregular stems — a sure sign that they were grown in the fields and not in a hothouse.*

1. Wash and pat dry the eggplants. Light two burners on the stove, keeping the heat low; and place an eggplant directly on the heat source (a gas flame is better than electric heat, but either will work). Leave the eggplants there, turning occasionally, until their skin begins to char and peel away, 10 to 15 minutes total. Remove the eggplants and cool them for just a few minutes. (They have to be hot when you peel and clean them.)

2. Pour the olive oil into a large bowl. Place one eggplant at a time on a piece of aluminum foil. Using a sharp knife, score the eggplant lengthwise down the middle. With the tip of the blade, carefully peel and slice away as much of the outer, charred, layer of skin as possible. Once the eggplant is open and the outer skin peeled away, score the pulp horizontally — this will make it easier to remove. Using a spoon, remove the pulp from the "inner" skin and submerge the pulp directly in the olive oil. Pick away any burnt flakes of skin that may have stuck to the pulp. Repeat with the second eggplant. Discard the skins.

3. Sprinkle salt to taste and a little sugar into the eggplant mixture and, using a fork or whisk, gently and slowly stir the eggplants round and round until they absorb all of the oil. This will take 8 to 10 minutes. The texture will be creamy and smooth, but not homogenous like a puree. Adjust seasoning with salt and lemon juice.

Serve warm or at room temperature.

Variation: If the smokiness of the eggplant cooked over raw heat isn't to your liking, then prick the eggplants with the tines of a fork and bake them in a hot oven (450°F), for about 45 minutes, or until the skin is soft and shriveled.

BREAD-AND-ALMOND DIPPING SAUCE

Skordalia me Amigdala kai Psomi

2 1-inch slices stale Italian or French bread, crusts removed

1/2 cup blanched almonds

4 to 6 large garlic cloves, peeled and crushed

2/3 to 3/4 cup extra-virgin olive oil

Strained juice of 1 large lemon, or more if necessary

Water, if necessary

Salt and pepper to taste

1. Run the bread under the tap to dampen, then squeeze it thoroughly dry and crumble it.

2. In a food processor, pulse the almonds on and off until they are mealy and granular. Add the garlic and pulse. Add the bread and pulse on and off, adding in turns the oil and lemon juice in a slow stream.

3. Taste the *skordalia,* season with salt and pepper, and additional lemon juice if desired. If it seems too thick, you can dilute it with a few tablespoons of water or additional oil or lemon juice.

Note: Pulse on and off cautiously, because if the bread is pulverized too rapidly the consistency will become starchy, almost gooey.

Yield: 6 to 8 servings

POTATO-GARLIC DIP WITH WALNUTS

Makedonitiki Skordalia

2 large potatoes, thoroughly washed

4 to 6 garlic cloves (to taste), peeled

1 cup chopped walnuts

Salt to taste

Strained fresh juice of 1 lemon

1/2 cup extra-virgin olive oil (or more, if necessary)

1/4 cup red wine vinegar

Yield: About 2 cups

1. Bring the potatoes to a boil in a large pot of water and simmer until tender, about 30 minutes.

2. Using a mortar and pestle, crush the garlic, one clove at a time, together with a little of the walnuts, salt, lemon juice, and olive oil. Remove the potatoes one at a time from the water and peel. Place the first potato in the mortar and pound, working the garlic-walnut mixture into it. Add olive oil, lemon juice, and vinegar alternating as you go. Add the second potato, peeled, and continue to work the mixture, adding more oil, lemon juice, vinegar, and seasonings if necessary until it is smooth and thick.

Note: Some cooks advocate pureeing the potatoes and the rest of the ingredients in a food processor, but the potatoes tend to break down too fast this way and become starchy and glutinous. An electric mixer with a paddle attachment works better, but pounding them by hand, although time-consuming, produces the best result.

"HARVEST" PUMPKIN-CHESTNUT-OLIVE PUREE FROM CRETE

Glykokolokitha me Kastana kai Elies

4 tablespoons extra-virgin olive oil

1 large leek, trimmed, washed, and finely chopped (about 2 cups)

4 garlic cloves, peeled, crushed, and chopped

1 large red bell pepper, seeded and finely chopped

1 red chili pepper or other small hot pepper (*e.g.,* Anaheim), seeded and chopped

5 cups peeled, seeded, and diced fresh sweet baking pumpkin (about 2 pounds, unpeeled)

1 1/2 cups boiled, peeled chestnuts, coarsely chopped

1/3 cup rinsed, pitted, and chopped cracked green olives (about 12 olives)

1/2 cup dry white wine

2 small heads radicchio or endive, leaves separated, rinsed, and dried

Salt to taste

The authentic version of this dish, which I first tasted at a restaurant in Herakleion, is made with something called xinohondro, *a lozenge-sized very hard buttermilk pasta, which is the local* trahana, *something difficult to find outside ethnic markets in America. It seemed like the kind of farm food that could be served in a posh restaurant, exactly the setting I was in when I encountered it. Everything in the fall garden is in this dish. Served on individual beds of radicchio or endive leaves it becomes surprisingly elegant.*

1. Heat the olive oil in a medium-sized pot and cook the leeks over low heat until soft, stirring, about 10 minutes. Add the garlic and peppers and continue cooking for another 5 to 7 minutes.

2. Add the pumpkin, cover the pot, and let the whole mixture cook in its own juices over low heat for 20 to 25 minutes, stirring occasionally, until the pumpkin is soft and more or less disintegrated. Check the pot occasionally and add water if necessary. Add the chestnuts and continue to simmer for another 10 minutes. Add the olives, and 1/4 cup water. Let the mixture simmer, uncovered and stirring it often, until it is as thick as oatmeal. Pour in the wine and cook for another 10 to 12 minutes. Remove pot from heat and drape a kitchen towel over it until the mixture cools. Serve the puree in spoon-size dollops on radicchio or endive leaves, and leave your dinner guests guessing.

Yield: About 3 cups

SALADS
BOTH RAW AND COOKED

A WORD ABOUT SALADS

It's encouraging to see the proliferation of farmer's markets throughout the United States, and to see that fresher looking vegetables (and a wider variety of them) are appearing on supermarket shelves. In Greece, we tend to take such things for granted—our cucumbers are crunchy, tomatoes linger with a sweet luscious aftertaste on the palate, herbs are truly flavorful, onions are extremely pungent and peppery. Perhaps it is this abundance of quality produce that makes salads such a mainstay in Greek cuisine, and yet the term "salad" is such a confusing one in Greek cooking. It can refer to a range of different dishes that have little in common with one another. Greeks call the dips and spreads in the previous chapter salads. They call boiled greens salad. They call raw vegetables dressed with olive oil and lemon juice or vinegar salad. The recipes that follow include both cooked and raw vegetable and bean salads.

HORTA – COOKED SALAD GREENS

Horta—it means simply *weed* in Greek, but it accounts for an enormous variety of edible wild greens that take a significant place on the country's vegetarian table. In Crete alone there are more than three hundred indigenous herbs and greens. Many are used medicinally, but many, too, find use in the kitchen.

Greens play a role in soups and stews, often in combination with legumes or with meat or fish. Sometimes they are stewed alone, as in an old recipe from Crete for stewed nettles, or as in a dish from the Ionian islands for chard stewed with onions and tomatoes. Greens form an important part in the whole savory pie tradition—there are countless greens pies, which call for everything from poppy leaves to wild fennel to spinach to nettles. Sometimes, but not often, greens are eaten raw in salad. Mâche is a popular salad green in Crete, as are arugula and purslane.

Most often, though, greens are boiled and eaten at room temperature in the form of salad. There is a whole philosophy behind the way one is supposed to boil greens. Most cooks say that the pot lid has to be left slightly ajar, but there is avid debate as to whether the water that the greens are boiled in should be salted first or not.

There are sweet greens, among them spinach, Swiss chard, beet greens, amaranth, collards, and kale. There are peppery greens, also boiled and dressed simply with olive oil and either lemon juice or vinegar, and these include cresses, black mustard greens, various other mustard greens, and sorrel. In rural areas and even in cities close to rural areas, such as Herakleion in Crete, one is also likely to find the buds and blossoms of many different plants, which Greek cooks also boil and dress for salad. These might include the young spring shoots of the grape vine, called *ambelovlastara,* the green tender shoots of a certain variety of daisy, the thick stalks of zucchini, something akin to brocoli rabe, pea shoots, and even caper leaves, which are a delicacy in the Cyclades.

What might seem obscure on the American market is often found at the local farmer's market even in urban Greece, and among the greens that one might consider rare are several types of thistles, many different varieties of greens in the cabbage family, an Old-World green known as centaury (or *askolimbri* in Crete), stinging nettles, kohlrabi leaves, wild asparagus, fiddlehead ferns, mallow, and lamb's lettuce, or mâche. Bitter greens number plenty, too, and among the ones Greeks like most are dandelions, chicory, and escarole.

There is no real recipe for boiling greens. Greeks tend to like them very well cooked, but that is really a matter of taste. They should be washed very thoroughly and trimmed, but cooked more or less uncut in lightly salted boiling water. It used to be custom to drink the water from certain boiled greens, especially beet greens and amaranth. Boil the greens until tender, drain thoroughly, and dress with olive oil and either fresh lemon juice or vinegar.

MUSHROOM AND OLIVE SALAD

Salata me Manitaria kai Elies

1/4 cup extra-virgin olive oil

1 pound small button mushrooms, trimmed but whole (or halved if they are more than an inch in diameter)

1 garlic clove, peeled and minced

3/4 cup rinsed, pitted, and halved kalamata olives

2 to 3 teaspoons balsamic vinegar

1/2 teaspoon oregano

Pepper to taste

1/4 pound Cretan graviera, diced*

Yield: 4 servings

*Graviera is a sharp yellow table cheese made in many parts of Greece and available widely at Greek and specialty food shops across the United States. Any semi-soft but vibrant cheese can be used here; just keep in mind that the olives tend to be overpowering, so the cheese has to be able to stand up to them.

When we were invited to celebrate the ten-year anniversary of Strofyllia, one of the first wine bars in the heart of Athens's old commercial center, we were treated to, among other things, this tangy and unusual combination. The mushrooms and olives have almost the same texture, so the contrast in flavors seems all the more intense.

1. Heat 2 tablespoons of olive oil in a large skillet and cook the mushrooms and garlic, covered, for 5 to 7 minutes. They should still be firm. Remove and cool slightly.

2. In a medium-sized bowl, combine the mushrooms and their pan juices with the olives, balsamic vinegar, oregano, and pepper. Mix in the remaining olive oil. Let the salad rest, covered and at room temperature, for 30 minutes to an hour. Just before serving, toss in the graviera.

ROXANI'S EGG AND LENTIL SALAD

Oi Fakes Salata tis Roxanis

1/2 pound large lentils

1 medium-sized ripe tomato, seeds removed and diced

1 medium-sized bell pepper, seeds removed and coarsely chopped

1 large onion, coarsely chopped (about 1 cup)

2 scallions, trimmed and washed, cut into thin rounds

1 large garlic clove, peeled and minced

1/4 cup extra-virgin olive oil

2 to 4 tablespoons red wine vinegar

1 1/2 cups finely chopped fresh flat-leaf parsley

2 hard-boiled eggs, quartered

Salt to taste

Yield: 4 to 6 servings

Every second weekend last spring, Roxani Matsa, one of the few women in Greece who produces wine, held a party at her estate. I helped her cook, but she always presented a few dishes of her own as well. She called this salad lentil tabouleh, even though bulgur wheat is nowhere in sight. It is fresh and filling, and the combination of lentils and hard-boiled eggs surprisingly complementary.

1. Rinse and drain the lentils. Place them in a large pot covered with about two inches of water and bring to a boil. Simmer over gentle heat, uncovered, for 20 to 25 minutes, until the lentils are tender but al dente. As they simmer, skim the foam from the surface. Drain and cool.

2. In a large salad bowl, combine the lentils with the diced tomato, pepper, onion, scallion, and garlic. Toss to combine. Add olive oil and vinegar and toss again. Garnish with parsley and hard-boiled eggs and serve immediately.

CLASSIC LENTIL SALAD

Fakes Salata

1/2 pound baby lentils

1 bay leaf

2 medium-sized onions, peeled and finely chopped (about 1 1/3 cups)

2 garlic cloves, peeled and chopped

1 large carrot, peeled and diced

1 cup finely chopped flat-leaf parsley

4 to 5 tablespoons extra-virgin olive oil

2 tablespoons red wine vinegar

Salt and black pepper to taste

1. Rinse the lentils and drain in a colander. Place in a pot with the bay leaf and ample water to cover by 2 to 3 inches. Bring to a boil, reduce heat, and simmer, uncovered, until the lentils are tender but firm, about 20 minutes. As they simmer, skim the foam from the surface. Remove to a colander, discard the bay leaf, rinse under cold water, and drain.

2. Toss the onion, garlic, and carrot with the lentils in a large serving bowl. Mix in the parsley and season to taste with olive oil, vinegar, salt, and pepper. Let stand, covered, for 30 minutes at room temperature before serving.

Yield: 4 to 6 servings

LENTIL SALAD WITH ROASTED RED PEPPERS AND FETA

Fakes Salata me Psites Piperies kai Feta

1 pound large lentils

6 scallions, cut into thin rounds

2 garlic cloves, minced

1 pound red bell peppers, roasted, seeded, peeled, and julienned

Salt and black pepper to taste

1/2 cup extra-virgin olive oil

3 to 4 tablespoons red wine vinegar

1/4 cup chopped dill

1/2 pound feta, crumbled

This fresh take on lentils, one of the most popular legumes in the Greek pot, comes from a Cretan friend and chef, Chris Veneris.

1. Rinse the lentils in a colander and drain. Place in a pot with ample water, heat, and simmer for 10 minutes. Remove, drain, and rinse in a colander under cold water.

2. Place back in pot with fresh water, bring to a boil, reduce heat, and simmer for 20 to 25 minutes, until tender but not mushy. As lentils simmer, skim foam from the surface. Remove, drain in a colander, and rinse under cold water.

3. In a large bowl, combine lentils, scallions, garlic, and peppers. Add salt, pepper, olive oil, and vinegar. Let stand for 30 minutes before serving. Serve at room temperature, topped with dill and crumbled feta.

Yield: 6 to 8 servings

SPICY LENTIL AND WILD RICE SALAD

Fakes Salata me Agrio Rizi

1 cup wild rice, rinsed and soaked for 30 minutes

1 cup baby lentils, rinsed and drained

1/4 cup plus 2 tablespoons extra-virgin olive oil

2 medium-sized carrots, washed, peeled, and diced

2 celery ribs, washed, trimmed, and minced

2 garlic cloves, peeled and minced

1 teaspoon ground cumin seeds

Salt and freshly ground black pepper to taste

2 to 3 tablespoons sherry vinegar

1. Drain the rice and place in a medium-sized pot with 4 cups of salted water. Bring to a boil, reduce heat, and simmer, covered, for about 40 minutes, or until the rice is tender. Remove and drain.

2. While rice is cooking, place the lentils in a medium-sized pot and cover them with 2 inches of water. Bring to a boil, reduce heat, and simmer, uncovered, until tender but al dente, about 20 minutes. As the lentils simmer, skim the foam from the surface. Remove, drain in a colander, and rinse under cold water.

3. While the lentils and rice are simmering, heat 3 tablespoons of the olive oil in a skillet and sauté the carrots and the celery for 6 to 7 minutes, until tender but al dente. Add the garlic and cumin seeds and stir for another minute. Remove from heat.

4. Place the wild rice, lentils, and vegetables in a medium-sized serving bowl, and toss to combine. Season with remaining olive oil, salt, pepper, and sherry vinegar. Let stand for 1 hour before serving.

Yield: 4 to 6 servings

THE SIMPLEST BLACK-EYED PEA SALAD

Gyftofasoula Salata

1/2 pound dried black-eyed peas, soaked according to package directions

1 bay leaf

Salt and coarsely ground black pepper

1 large red onion, peeled, halved, and sliced

1/3 cup extra-virgin olive oil

2 tablespoons red wine vinegar (or more, to taste)

Yield: 4 to 6 servings

Black-eyed peas are called "gypsy beans" in Greece. In some parts of the country, especially in Nyssiros, an island in the eastern Aegean, you can find them fresh in the pod in spring, in which case they are cooked al dente in a light fresh tomato sauce. This recipe calls for dried beans and represents the way Greeks like so many of their bean salads—boiled and dressed laconically with extra-virgin olive oil, red onions, and vinegar. The trick here is really in the onions. They should be cut not into paper-thin translucent slices, but rather into thick crescent-shaped slices that let you savor their texture.

1. Wash and drain the beans. Place them in a pot with the bay leaf and enough water to cover them by 2 to 3 inches. Bring to a boil, reduce heat, and simmer for about 30 minutes, until the beans are tender but al dente. Pour them out into a colander and rinse under cold water. Drain thoroughly.

2. Place the beans in a serving bowl. Season to taste with salt and pepper. Garnish with the onion and toss with the olive oil and vinegar. Let stand for 15 minutes before serving.

Fava with Sun-Dried Tomatoes and Capers (page 38)

Spicy Lentil and Wild Rice Salad
(page 51)

Diporto's Greek Villager's Salad
(page 55)

Barley Rusk Salad with Grated Tomato and Herbs (page 56)
Bulgur and Chick-Pea Pilaf (page 87)

BLACK-EYED PEA SALAD
WITH CELERY AND CUMIN

Pikantiki Mavromatika Salata

1/2 pound dried black-eyed peas, soaked according to package directions

1/3 cup extra-virgin olive oil

2 celery ribs, trimmed and diced

2 garlic cloves, peeled and minced

1 teaspoon cumin seeds

1/4 teaspoon mustard seeds

3 scallions, trimmed and cut into thin rounds

Salt and freshly ground black pepper to taste

Dash of cayenne

2 to 4 tablespoons strained fresh lemon juice

1. Wash and drain the beans. Place them in a pot with enough water to cover them by 2 to 3 inches. Bring to a boil, reduce heat, and simmer for about 30 minutes, until they are tender but al dente. Pour them out into a colander and rinse under cold water. Drain thoroughly.

2. Heat 2 tablespoons of the olive oil in a small skillet and sauté the celery and garlic for 2 to 3 minutes. Add the cumin seeds and mustard seeds. Heat and toss all together another 1 to 2 minutes, just to bring out the flavor of the spices.

3. In a large salad bowl, combine the black-eyed peas with the celery mixture and scallions. Season with salt, pepper, and cayenne. Add remaining olive oil and lemon juice. Let the salad sit for at least an hour at room temperature before serving.

Yield: 4 to 6 servings

ROASTED EGGPLANT AND CHICK-PEA SALAD

Melitzana Psiti me Revithia

2 medium-sized eggplants
(about 2 pounds total)

Salt

3/4 cup olive oil

1 cup cooked chick-peas
(canned are fine)

2 garlic cloves, peeled and
finely chopped

1 large, firm ripe tomato,
peeled, seeded, and diced

1 teaspoon dried oregano

Salt and freshly ground
black pepper to taste

2 to 3 tablespoons strained
fresh lemon juice

1/4 cup crumbled feta
(optional)

In parts of northern Greece, eggplants stewed or baked for hours in a clay pot with chick-peas is a common dish. Here, the basic ingredients are the same, only the recipe is lighter, easier, and quicker to make.

1. Trim the stems and bottoms off the eggplants. Cut in half lengthwise and then dice into 3/4-inch cubes. Place the eggplant in a colander and sprinkle each layer generously with salt. Place a weight (such as a pot cover) over the eggplant and let it drain for 30 minutes. Rinse and drain well, squeezing gently to remove excess liquid, and pat dry.

2. Heat 1/4 cup of olive oil in a large skillet and sauté half the eggplant, tossing gently, over medium heat until lightly browned and tender, but not mushy. Remove, cool slightly, and repeat with remaining eggplant and 1/4 cup of oil.

3. In a large bowl, combine the eggplant with the chick-peas, garlic, diced tomato, and oregano. Adjust seasoning with salt and pepper. Add lemon juice and remaining olive oil and let the salad stand, covered, at room temperature to marinate for at least 1 hour before serving.

Optional: Toss in 1/4 cup of crumbled feta.

Yield: 2 to 4 servings

DIPORTO'S GREEK VILLAGER'S SALAD

Horiatiki Salata

3 large, firm ripe tomatoes

1 large red onion, peeled

1 small cucumber, peeled and sliced into 1/8-inch rounds

1 large green pepper, seeded, halved, and sliced thin

1 to 2 long, thin hot green peppers, seeded and cut into thin rounds

1/2 cup kalamata olives

1/4 cup extra-virgin olive oil

Salt to taste

2 to 3 pinches of dried oregano

1/3 pound feta (optional)

Yield: 4 servings

Villager's salad is the classic Greek salad—ripe tomatoes, sliced onion, crunchy peppers and cucumbers, kalamata olives, feta, and extra-virgin olive oil. Diporto is a small taverna, open for lunch only, on the perimeter of the Athens Central Market. The cook and owner, Mitso, prepares all the classics of simple country Greek fare, as well as the best horiatiki salata in the city. His secret: the unabashed addition of hot green peppers.

1. Wash and dry the tomatoes. Cut them in half lengthwise, core them, and cut each half into thirds or quarters. Cut the onion the same way, halved and then into chunky wedges.

2. Toss the tomatoes, onion, cucumber, peppers, and olives together in a serving bowl. Add olive oil, salt, and oregano and serve immediately.

Optional: Crumble a little feta over the salad just before serving.

BARLEY RUSK SALAD WITH GRATED TOMATO AND HERBS

Kritiko Dako

2 doughnut-shaped Cretan barley rusks

1 large, ripe, firm tomato

1/4 pound feta, crumbled

2 teaspoons dried oregano or basil

Freshly ground black pepper to taste

3 to 4 tablespoons extra-virgin olive oil

Yield: 2 to 4 servings

Rusks prevail in the country breadmaking traditions throughout Greece. Home bakers used to make bread in their own, usually outdoor, ovens about once a week, and the making of rusks were part of the ritual. Slow-baked and hard, they were a way to preserve bread for the days when the household might be short of it, and have always been a convenient food for the fields. Drizzled with a little water to soften them and then seasoned with olive oil, rusks in many shapes and sizes and from various grains were and are the lunchtime snack of farmers. In Crete, the beautiful, dark, doughnut-shaped rusks are called dako, *and they are usually made from barley. They are widely available in Greek stores throughout America.*

As for the tomato, this recipe calls for grating them, which is something Greek cooks are quite inured to. It's an easy way to make an instant concassé.

1. Run the rusks under the tap for a few seconds to dampen. Break up into four large pieces and place on a plate or small platter.

2. Wash and dry the tomato. Hold from the stem end and grate onto a plate. Spoon the grated tomato, juices and all, over the rusks. Sprinkle with feta, oregano, pepper, and olive oil and let stand at room temperature for 20 minutes before serving.

SAMOS PLUM TOMATO AND PURSLANE SALAD

Bournelosalata

2 pounds small, firm plum tomatoes or cherry tomatoes, washed

1 bunch purslane (about 1/4 pound)

2 medium-sized red onions, peeled and coarsely chopped

2 small cucumbers, peeled and sliced thin

1 small green hot pepper

1/3 cup chopped flat-leaf parsley

Extra-virgin olive oil

Oregano, salt, and pepper to taste

Some parts of Greece claim varieties of tomatoes all their own. Santorini has its tiny anydra, *or "waterless" tomatoes; Chios boasts its own small round tomatoes, which are left to dry in bunches from the rafters of every home and taverna all summer long; and Samos has the* bournelo, *a similarly small, very intense-flavored tomato that is used in islanders' favorite salad. Purslane appears at the end of summer in Greece and usually is available through the middle of fall. It is called* glistrida *(slippery) because folk wisdom has it that the thick-stemmed green makes people especially talkative, or slippery-tongued!*

1. Core the tomatoes. If using cherries, halve them; if using plum tomatoes, quarter them. Trim the purslane: Cut away the thick tough bottom part of the stems and use only the leaves and tender thin stems for the salad.

2. Combine the tomatoes, purslane, onions, cucumbers, hot pepper, and parsley in a serving bowl. Add olive oil, oregano, salt, and pepper to taste and toss. Serve immediately.

Yield: About 6 servings

GREEK DELI SLAW

Politiki Lahanosalata

2 cups finely shredded white cabbage

2 cups finely shredded red cabbage

2 cups peeled and finely shredded carrot

4 roasted red peppers, seeded and finely chopped (about 1 1/4 cups)

2 tablespoons tiny capers

1 garlic clove

1/3 cup finely chopped flat-leaf parsley

1/3 cup extra-virgin olive oil

2 tablespoons red wine vinegar

1 tablespoon coarse-grain Dijon mustard

Salt to taste

Although the word "deli" has a snobbish connotation in modern-day Greece, the concept is as old as the agora. Shops that sell takeout mezes—prepared salads, a savory pie or two, dips—also sell dozens of different olives, smoked and brine-cured fish and charcuterie, cheeses, pickled vegetables, and everything else the traditional Greek food lover wants on her table. Among the salads will frequently be this colorful cabbage slaw, not sweet like the American kind, but tart and briny with vinegar and capers. The trick is in shredding the cabbages and the carrots as fine as, or finer than, matchsticks. I use what's known in the trade as a mandoline for the shredding—an upright stainless steel or plastic kitchen tool that has a stationary blade as well as a removable comblike blade for shredding.

1. Combine all the ingredients except the oil, vinegar, mustard, and salt in a large salad bowl and toss with a fork to combine.

2. Whisk together the remaining ingredients for the dressing, pour over the salad, toss, and serve immediately.

Yield: 6 servings

VASSILIS'S CABBAGE SALAD

Lahanosalata tou Vassilis

4 cups shredded white cabbage, washed and thoroughly drained

2 garlic cloves, peeled and minced

1/2 cup snipped fresh dill

1/4 cup extra-virgin olive oil

2 teaspoons grainy Dijon mustard

1 tablespoon plain yogurt

2 teaspoons strained fresh lemon juice

Salt and freshly ground black pepper to taste

Yield: 4 servings

My husband, Vassilis, does two things exceedingly well in the kitchen—he has a light hand with the fryer and a great touch with salads. This simple cabbage salad is a winter standard on our table. The garlic lends a rich but subtle undertone to the otherwise mellow cabbage.

1. Combine the cabbage, garlic, and dill in a serving bowl. Toss to mix.

2. In a small bowl or jar, whisk or shake together the olive oil, mustard, yogurt, and lemon juice until the dressing is smooth and creamy. Pour into the salad just before serving, and season to taste with salt and pepper.

ARUGULA SALAD WITH WRINKLED OLIVES AND ORANGE SLICES

Roka Salata me Throumbes kai Portokali

2 small bunches arugula, trimmed, washed, and spun dry

1 small navel orange, halved horizontally

1 cup Greek throumbes (wrinkled black olives)

1 medium-sized red onion, peeled, halved, and sliced

1/4 cup extra-virgin olive oil

2 tablespoons sherry vinegar

1/2 teaspoon dried oregano or thyme

Salt and freshly ground black pepper to taste

Yield: 4 servings

Arugula — roka to the Greeks — is one of the commonest winter greens. It grows wild in gardens and fields and is the standard winter salad in several islands, most notably Andros, during the festive period of the hirosfagia, or pig slaughter, which takes place in rural Greece around Christmas and on the saints' days before and after.

1. Tear the arugula by hand into large pieces. Place in a serving bowl. Peel one half of the orange and dice it. Toss the arugula with the orange bits, olives, and onion.

2. Juice the other half of the orange and whisk it together with the olive oil, vinegar, oregano, salt, and pepper. Just before serving, dress the salad.

THE GREEK VEGETARIAN

WARM MEZES

A WORD ON WARM MEZES

Most of these dishes are meant to be prepared and eaten immediately. They represent the kind of food one can whip up without much notice, to accommodate, say, an unexpected guest or as a quick dinner. Many of the recipes that follow require frying, something Greek cooks do not hold in taboo. They simply indulge, but not in quantity, and typically use olive oil in the skillet.

TWO SAGANAKIS

(Pan-Fried Cheese)

The word *saganaki* actually refers to the double-handled shallow skillet in which this classic Greek *meze* is traditionally prepared.

SAGANAKI WITH SMOKED CHEESE AND PAPRIKA

2 to 3 tablespoons all-purpose flour

1/2 pound metsovone or smoked provolone, cut into 4 equal, round slices

4 teaspoons butter

Sweet paprika

Yield: 4 servings

Saganaki *can be made with almost any medium-to-hard cheese. The most common is kefalograviera, a slightly nutty yellow cheese made throughout the country. The following* saganaki *calls for a smoked cheese, metsovone, which is made at the cheese cooperative in the northwestern Greek town of Métsovon and can be found in Greek and Middle Eastern food shops across America. The cheese is not unlike smoked provolone, which can be used as a substitute. This particular version of* saganaki *is served locally in Métsovon's taverns.*

1. Spread flour on a plate. Run each slice of cheese under the tap, then dip lightly in the flour.

2. Heat half the butter in a small skillet and add the first slice of cheese. Panfry it over medium-low heat, turning it once, until it softens and browns and is just on the verge of melting. Remove the cooked slice from pan. Repeat with second slice. Heat the remaining butter and repeat with remaining two slices. Serve immediately, sprinkled with paprika.

AGROTIKON'S SAGANAKI

1 pound Greek graviera
cheese*

3 to 4 tablespoons flour

1 Red Delicious apple,
washed, cored, and halved

4 to 5 tablespoons butter

3 to 4 fresh sage leaves

1/2 cup apple cider or juice

1/4 cup ouzo

1/2 cup coarsely chopped
walnuts

Yield: 6 to 8 servings

*Graviera is a sharp yellow
table cheese made in many
parts of Greece and available widely at Greek and
specialty food shops across
the United States. Any semi-
soft but vibrant cheese can
be used in its place.

*Of the ten or so Greek restaurants that have recently opened in Manhat-
tan, one of my favorites is Agrotikon, on Fourteenth Street and First
Avenue. This saganaki, served with sautéed apples and walnuts, is a
takeoff on Agrotikon's.*

1. Cut the cheese in half and then into rectangular slices about 1/4
inch thick. Run under the tap and then dredge lightly with flour. Set
aside until ready to use.

2. Cut the apple into thin crescent-shaped slices. Heat 2 tablespoons
of butter in a medium-sized skillet and sauté the apples together with
the sage leaves until the apples are lightly browned but firm. Remove
the sage leaves.

3. Remove the apples to a serving platter and cover to keep warm.
Add remaining butter to the skillet and panfry the cheese, in batches if
necessary, turning it once. As soon as it is on the verge of melting, pour
in the apple juice and ouzo. In a minute or so the juices will thicken.
Remove the cheese to the serving platter, strew the apples all around,
and drizzle with the pan juices. Garnish with walnuts and serve immediately.

GRILLED GREEN PEPPERS STUFFED WITH FETA

Piperies Yemistes me Feta

1/2 pound Greek feta, crumbled

1 teaspoon cayenne

Freshly ground black pepper to taste

1 to 2 teaspoons dried thyme or oregano

1 to 2 tablespoons strained fresh lemon juice

1/3 cup plus 2 to 3 table-spoons olive oil

8 large, long green peppers, washed and dried

Yield: 4 to 8 servings

The best-loved meze *in Salonika. There is something about the sweet taste of peppers and the sour, tart taste of feta that marries exceptionally well. This is classic taverna fare, and a great buffet dish.*

1. Place the feta, cayenne, black pepper, thyme or oregano, lemon juice, and 1 to 2 tablespoons of the olive oil in the bowl of a food processor and whip for a few seconds until smooth.

2. Heat 1/3 cup olive oil in a large heavy skillet and sauté the peppers over high heat for about 1 minute on each side, or until the skin starts to puff. Remove with a slotted spoon and wrap loosely in a large sheet of aluminum foil.

3. Let the peppers steam in the foil for a few minutes, and when they are cool enough to handle, carefully cut off and reserve their lids. Gently scrape or pull out the seeds. Peel the peppers carefully so as not to tear.

4. Preheat the broiler and lightly oil a shallow baking pan large enough to hold the peppers in a single layer. Using a dull knife (such as a butter knife) or a pastry bag, fill the peppers with the cheese mixture, leaving about an inch of room at the top. Gently stuff the lids back into each of the peppers. Place the peppers 6 to 8 inches from the heat and broil for 3 to 5 minutes, until the cheese melts and the peppers begin to brown lightly. Serve immediately.

POTATO PATTIES WITH FRESH OREGANO

Riganokeftedes

2 pounds potatoes, peeled and washed

1/4 pound fresh oregano

1 large onion, peeled and finely chopped

Salt and freshly ground pepper to taste

1 large egg

2/3 to 1 cup plain bread crumbs (or more, if necessary)

All-purpose flour

Oil for frying

Yield: About 30 patties

Fresh herbs, with the exception of mint, dill, and parsley, are rarely used in Greek cooking. Greeks prefer dried herbs instead. This dish, from Mount Pelion in Thessaly, is one of the few that call for fresh oregano. It is usually made only in the late spring, when oregano is in bloom.

1. Bring the potatoes to a boil in ample salted water and simmer, uncovered, over medium heat until soft, about 20 minutes.

2. Using your thumb and forefinger, draw down on the oregano stems to remove the leaves. Discard the stems. Submerge the leaves in a small bowl of water to wash, swish around, and remove by the handful. Bring a small pot of water to a rolling boil and submerge the oregano, blanching it for just a minute. Strain and set aside to cool slightly. Squeeze the oregano between your palms to wring out excess moisture and finely chop, either by hand or in a food processor.

3. When the potatoes are soft, drain them and allow to cool slightly. Mash them by hand, while still hot, with a fork or potato masher. Add the oregano and chopped onion. Season with salt and pepper and mix in the egg. Knead the mixture to combine well, adding a little bit of the bread crumbs at a time until the mixture is substantial enough to be formed into patties without falling apart. Test seasoning and add salt if needed.

4. Spread flour on a large plate. Taking about 1 heaping tablespoon at a time of the mashed potato mixture, shape into flat little patties, approximately 1 1/2 inches in diameter. Flour on both sides. Heat 1 inch of oil in a large heavy skillet and fry the patties in batches. Flip to brown on both sides, remove with a slotted spoon, and drain on paper towels.

Serve warm or at room temperature.

WILD GREENS OR SPINACH FRITTERS

Hortokeftedes

2 pounds fresh spinach, or other greens such as dandelion or chard

1 large red onion, peeled and quartered

Salt and freshly ground black pepper to taste

1 scant teaspoon freshly grated nutmeg

1 1/2 cups all-purpose flour

1 teaspoon baking powder

1 1/2 to 2 cups water

1 egg, slightly beaten

Olive or other vegetable oil for frying

Yield: 6 to 8 servings

Vegetable fritters are made all over Greece, with all manner of greens, from common spinach to more exotic dandelion, sorrel, and amaranth. I love this dish because, like so much of Greek cooking, it mirrors the economy of the home cook. Greens are free for the picking in Greece. They have always provided a major source of nutrition, and the fact that they are prepared in so many different ways—boiled for salad, baked into savory pies, cooked with fish and meat in combination stews, and, finally, turned into substantial fritters like the ones below—reflects the ingenuity of country cooking. Greeks are not shy about frying, and these fritters are usually the star attraction of a meze *table or a makeshift meal, most often served with a bowl of strong* skordalia *or* tzatziki.

1. Trim the stems off the greens and discard. Coarsely chop the greens and wash as for lettuce or other salad greens—by submerging in water and removing several times, until all the grit is gone. Spin dry or drain thoroughly in a colander. Place the spinach in a vegetable steamer and steam for about 3 minutes, just until tender. Remove and drain.

2. Using a food processor, pulverize the onion to a juicy pulp. Combine the steamed spinach with the onion and season with salt, pepper, and nutmeg.

3. To make the batter, Combine the flour with the baking powder and 1/2 teaspoon of salt. Make a well in center and add 1 1/2 cups of water and the beaten egg. Mix thoroughly. The batter should be fairly thick. Toss the spinach and onion mixture in with the batter and mix to combine thoroughly.

4. Heat 2 inches of oil in a large heavy skillet. When it is just below the smoking point, begin to fry the fritters, several at a time. Take a tablespoon or small ladleful of the spinach batter and drop it into the skillet, just as you would with pancake batter. As soon as the fritters brown on one side, flip them to cook on the other. Drain on paper towels, and continue until all the batter is used up, adding more oil if necessary during the process.

PUMPKIN-POTATO PATTIES

Keftedes apo Kolokitha kai Patates

2 pounds sweet baking pumpkin, seeds and rind removed, coarsely chopped

1 pound potatoes, peeled and cut into chunks

1 large red onion, minced

1 to 2 eggs, slightly beaten

2 tablespoons dried mint

Salt and freshly ground black pepper to taste

2 to 4 tablespoons plain bread crumbs (optional)

Flour for dredging

Vegetable oil for frying

Yield: 6 to 8 servings

1. Place the pumpkin in a vegetable steamer in a pot with about 1 inch of water and steam until very tender. You should be able to mash the pumpkin easily with a fork.

2. Place the potatoes in a large pot with enough water to cover by 1 inch, bring to a boil, and simmer until the potatoes are tender enough for a fork to split them easily. Remove and peel.

3. Place the pumpkin and potatoes in a large mixing bowl and mash together with a potato masher until pureed. Add the onion and 1 egg and combine. Add more egg if the mixture seems too compact. Add the mint, salt, and pepper and mix thoroughly. The mixture should be substantial enough to form into small patties. If at this point it seems loose, sprinkle in a few tablespoons of the bread crumbs.

4. Take 1 heaping tablespoon of the mixture at a time and shape into small patties, about 1/2 inch thick and 1 1/2 inches in diameter. Heat 1 inch of vegetable oil in a large skillet. Spread about half a cup of flour on a large plate and lightly dredge the patties. Fry them, a few at a time, in the hot oil, turning once, until they are golden brown. Remove and drain on paper towels. Serve hot, with *skordalia* or with plain (preferably strained) yogurt.

FRIED PUMPKIN WITH SKORDALIA

Tiganiti Kolkitha me Skordalia

1 pound sweet baking pumpkin (such a small amount
will probably mean buying a
portion of a pumpkin)

1/3 cup all-purpose flour

Salt and freshly ground
black pepper to taste

Olive or other oil for frying

1 recipe for *skordalia* (see
page 43)

Yield: 6 to 8 servings

Pumpkin comes to market in Greece in early October and lasts all winter. This is a favorite island dish, found readily in Crete and in the eastern Aegean. Elsewhere around the country, pumpkin is often used to make small patties, with flour or potatoes, eggs, and mint (see preceding recipe). I like this simple recipe because the flavor of the squash is blatant, and the color a beautiful reminder of winter looming.

1. Scrape out and discard the pumpkin seeds.

2. Depending on the shape of the pumpkin, cut it so that you have wide rectangular strips, which will make peeling the tough skin easy. Place each piece on its side and cut away the shell with a sharp butcher's knife. Cut the pumpkin into thin wide strips.

3. Place the strips in a colander and salt each layer lightly. Let drain for 1 hour.

4. Heat about 1 inch of olive oil in a large heavy skillet. Toss the flour, salt, and pepper together on a plate and lightly coat the pumpkin on both sides with the flour. Fry in hot oil until golden, remove, and drain on paper towels. Serve piping hot on a platter surrounding a pungent bowl of *skordalia*.

GRILLED MUSHROOMS WITH OREGANO AND OLIVE OIL

Psita Agria Manitaria me Rigani kai Lathi

6 to 8 large oyster mush-rooms, stems trimmed

2 teaspoons extra-virgin olive oil

1 garlic clove, peeled and minced

Salt and freshly ground black pepper to taste

1 to 2 teaspoons sherry vinegar or strained fresh lemon juice

Pinch of Greek oregano

Yield: 4 to 6 servings

Greek cooks do one of several things to mushrooms wild and tame. They pickle them, sometimes they stew them, but when assigned to the meze plate they love to grill them over coals and serve them up sizzling hot with lemon juice and herbs. In this case, the grill is a cast-iron skillet set over high heat. The mushrooms sear and brown but retain all their delicious juices.

1. Wash the mushrooms and pat dry.

2. Heat 1 teaspoon of the olive oil in a large cast-iron skillet. Add half the garlic, stir and brown, then remove with a slotted spoon. Add half the mushrooms to the skillet and sear over medium-high heat, turning, until lightly browned. Season with salt and pepper and remove to a serving platter. Repeat with remaining oil, garlic, and mushrooms. Sprinkle the mushrooms with sherry vinegar or lemon juice and oregano. Serve hot.

ROASTED BEETS WITH SKORDALIA

Patzaria Psita me Skordalia

4 large beets

2 large garlic cloves, crushed and peeled

1 teaspoon allspice berries

1/2 to 1 teaspoon black peppercorns

Salt to taste

6 to 8 tablespoons extra-virgin olive oil

1 tablespoon balsamic vinegar

1 recipe for *skordalia* (see page 43)

Boiled beet salad with a side dish of skordalia *is pretty standard fare at home and in tavernas around Greece. This recipe adds two twists: spices and baking, to enhance the earthiness of the beets.*

1. Scrub the beets and trim off their stem and root ends. Peel with a vegetable peeler and cut into 1/4-inch rounds.

2. Crush the garlic, allspice berries, peppercorns, and salt using a mortar and pestle, so that the mixture becomes pastelike and damp. Place the beets in a shallow ovenproof glass or ceramic bowl and toss with the spice mixture, the olive oil, and the vinegar. Let stand, covered, for 1 hour to marinate.

3. Preheat oven to 400°F. Cover the dish and bake the beets until tender, about 50 minutes, turning occasionally. Remove and serve immediately with a side of *skordalia.*

Yield: 2 to 4 servings

EGGPLANT BAKED WITH OREGANO AND MINT

Melitzana Riganata

3 medium eggplants (about 2 1/2 pounds total)

Salt

1/3 cup extra-virgin olive oil

1/4 cup sherry vinegar

1 tablespoon dried oregano

1 garlic clove, peeled and chopped

Salt and freshly ground black pepper

1/4 cup finely chopped fresh mint

1/3 cup grated Parmesan or Greek kefalograviera

Yield: 4 to 6 servings

This recipe for eggplant comes from a small restaurant in Plaka called Daphne's.

1. Trim the stems and bottoms off the eggplants. Peel the eggplants and cut them in half across the middle (not lengthwise). Cut each half vertically into four 1/4- 1/2-inch slices. Place the eggplant in a colander and sprinkle generously with salt. Place a weight (such as a pot cover) over the eggplant and let drain for 1 hour.

2. Preheat oven to 350°F. Rinse the eggplant and drain well, then pat dry. In a large clay or ovenproof glass baking dish, toss the eggplant with olive oil, vinegar, oregano, garlic, salt, and pepper. Cover with aluminum foil and bake for 1 hour, tossing occasionally to keep eggplant from sticking to dish. The eggplant will be very tender.

3. Remove from oven and toss with chopped mint. Adjust seasoning and serve topped with grated cheese.

PEPPERS COOKED IN OLIVE OIL WITH ONIONS

Piperonata

2 pounds mixed green, red, yellow, and orange bell peppers

1/4 cup extra-virgin olive oil

2 large onions, peeled, halved, and cut into thin slices

1 large garlic clove, peeled and minced

Salt to taste

3 to 4 tablespoons strong red wine vinegar

Yield: 6 to 8 servings

We tasted this dish at a friend's house one Clean Monday—the first day of Lent on the Greek Orthodox calendar. It is by no means a traditional Lenten dish, but it fits the bill—perfect vegetarian fare, healthful, and delicious. It is the Greek answer to roasted red peppers, a mixture of colored peppers cut into thin strips and cooked in their own juices until soft. It looks great served in a large clay bowl, and is perfect on a buffet table.

1. Wash and drain the peppers. Wipe them dry. Cut away the stems and cut the peppers in half lengthwise. Remove the seeds and pith. Cut the peppers into thin strips (about 1/8 inch wide) across the width.

2. Heat the olive oil in a large skillet and cook the onions over low heat until they wilt and begin to caramelize, about 10 minutes. Add the garlic and stir for a few seconds. Add the peppers and toss to coat with oil. Let the peppers cook, stirring occasionally, for 20 to 25 minutes, until they are quite soft. Season with salt and sprinkle with vinegar. Toss, place in a bowl, and let cool to room temperature before serving.

HOT GREEN PEPPERS SAUTÉED WITH TOMATO

Kafteres Piperies me Tomata

1/2 cup olive oil, or more if necessary

1 1/2 pounds Anaheim peppers

3 to 4 garlic cloves, peeled and minced

1 cup peeled, chopped plum tomatoes

3 to 4 tablespoons chopped fresh flat-leaf parsley

Yield: 3 to 4 servings

This dish, another classic from Crete, is made with a variety of thick-skinned slim green peppers that I have not seen in America. The closest is the mildly hot Anaheim. It works with Italian peppers, too, except that their thin filmlike skin puffs up unpleasantly during cooking — Italian peppers need to be peeled once they are fried. It also works with the common green bell pepper — just seed it first and cut it into 1 1/2-inch strips. Regardless of the type of pepper you choose, the simplicity of this dish is what makes it so good.

1. Wash and dry the peppers thoroughly. Warm the olive oil in a large heavy skillet over medium heat for 1 minute. Add the peppers, cover the skillet, and let the peppers cook slowly, turning them over, until they are softened and slightly browned. This should take 7 to 10 minutes.

2. Remove the peppers with a slotted spoon, reserving as much of the oil and juices as possible in the pan. Cook the garlic in the same oil for 2 to 3 minutes, over medium heat, stirring, and add the tomatoes. Let them simmer, stirring occasionally until thick, about 10 minutes. Place the peppers back in the skillet and cook all together for 5 more minutes. Serve warm or at room temperature, sprinkled with chopped parsley.

Variation: For eggplant in tomato sauce, cut 2 large long eggplants into 1/2-inch round slices. Salt and drain in a colander for 30 minutes, pat dry, and fry, then cook as above.

MAIN MEALS

PASTA AND OTHER GRAIN DISHES

I will never forget walking into a tiny general store in a small mountain village on Chios a few summers ago and seeing the grandfather hull wheat by hand at a wooden table by the only window in the shop. I had gone to the village in search of local cheese, and discovered another local specialty: handmade pasta. There are dozens of traditional pastas in Greece, all homemade and all different from place to place. In Ithaca, for example, there is something called *nioki,* which has nothing to do with its Italian homonym but is rather handmade orzo. In Crete, women still take care to hand-roll pencil-thin strips of dough for *skioufihta,* a slightly twisted or indented local pasta that is about as large as a small finger. This pasta is used in a fall and winter dish, eaten usually with a rich tomato sauce that sometimes includes snails. Another Cretan pasta, the *hilofta,* which is essentially an egg noodle, is served with honey to new mothers in order to help them enrich their milk for nursing. The obscure is vast in Greece!

The two most common pasta varieties again change shape and form from place to place. Greek egg noodles, or *hilopittes* (the word literally translates as "batter pies"), are sometimes long and flat like fettuccine, sometimes flat and wide like traditional American egg noodles, or tiny and square, or flat and short and curled. Greeks like them well-cooked, soft, and swimming in sauce. I have included one recipe for egg noodles with tahini sauce in this chapter.

The other traditional Greek pasta product, which is usually reserved for soups, is *trahana. Trahana* is a tiny granular pasta made with flour and either buttermilk, yogurt, or vegetable pulp at the end of the summer in rural Greece. Once the dough is made, it is broken into large chunks and left to dry in the shade for several days, and then broken again or milled into its small pebblelike final form. In Crete, *trahana* is called *xinohondro*—which means sour chunk—exactly what it is there, a larger and bulkier form of *trahana* than is found in other parts of the country. The Cretan version is made by soaking bulgur in buttermilk, then shaping it into chunks. In Lesvos the same pasta is shaped like small, flat cups. Although I have reserved the *trahana* recipes for the soup chapter, I thought it necessary to include a word on this unusual pasta here. It is made commercially and is easy to find in Greek and Middle Eastern food shops, where it comes in two varieties—sweet, which is made with whole milk, and sour, which is made with either yogurt or buttermilk.

Bulgur wheat and rice make up the two other major grain products cooked in the Greek kitchen. Bulgur is found, of course, all over the Near East, but especially in countries where wheat is produced. Making it is a fascinating process. Essentially, the wheat kernels are steeped in boiling water, then dried and milled into various grinds. The hot water penetrates the seeds, dissolving some of the vitamins and nutrients in the outer bran layer and carrying them inside the grain. The hot water also helps to gelatinize the starch granules and kills any germs or larvae that might be present. Once the wheat seeds are boiled, they are spread in the sun to dry or baked in a slow oven. The dried seeds are then sprayed with water in order to facilitate the removal of the outer bran layer, which in old times was done by rubbing the seeds together but now is done with special abrasion machines. The peeled grains are spread out again to dry, and finally ground into various grades, from coarse to fine.

In Greece, bulgur appears in many different recipes. It was a staple in the winter diet of Epirote Jews. In Macedonia, there is an interesting recipe, which Paula Wolfert includes in *The Cooking of the Eastern Mediterranean*, for grape leaves stuffed with bulgur, broad beans, and dried black figs. In Crete, bulgur is consumed widely in pilafs and stuffings, and one of the island's classics is a zucchini and bulgur pilaf. In Cyprus, bulgur is the rural convenience food—the kind of dish you might prepare on the spur of the moment to accommodate unexpected guests. Cypriots cook bulgur with lentils and tomatoes. Among the Greeks of the East, especially the Greeks of the Poli, or Istanbul, bulgur is the king of grains. They may have learned to appreciate it from the Turks, who eat great quantities of bulgur. In any event, some of the most flavorful recipes for what is otherwise a rather neutral food come from the Greeks of Asia Minor. I have included several here.

Rice in the Greek kitchen is used in soups and stuffings, in pilafs, and in long-simmered risotto-like dishes with spinach, cabbage, leeks, or tomatoes. There are several kinds of rice, each with its specific role in the larder. The long-simmered dishes, one of which I have included here, usually call for *rizi nihaki*, which is simply long-grain rice. Stuffed dishes and soups usually require a short-grain polished rice, which Greeks call *glacé*. All the rice recipes included here call for either long-grain, basmati, or (in one recipe) wild rice, the last two being recent additions to the Greek supermarket shelf, but ones that have been enthusiastically embraced.

Corn has a stormy relationship with the Greek table. Nowadays, few people cook with cornmeal. The exception is in the cuisine of northwestern Greece, where cornmeal is used as a crust for several savory greens pies and also baked into sweet cakes soaked in syrup. Corn used to be so closely associated with dire poverty that cooks have more or less eschewed it, but there are many old recipes for dishes similar to the Italian polenta. In the Ionian, corn mush actually is called polenta, evincing the region's long historical ties to Venice. Elsewhere, the same dish has many different names. I have included one here, called *katsamaki*, from Kardhitsa, in the center of mainland Greece.

The recipes that follow include several from Greece's rich and vibrant agricultural traditions. But I also opted for pragmatism. All of the pasta and grain recipes call for ingredients that are easily available to American cooks.

ZITI WITH CRANBERRY BEANS AND CELERY

Makaronaki Kofto me Barbounia

1/2 cup olive oil

1 cup coarsely chopped onion (about 1 medium-sized onion)

3 celery ribs, trimmed and cut horizontally into thin pieces (about 2 cups)

2 garlic cloves, peeled and minced

1 1/4 cups dried cranberry beans (approximately half a bag), soaked according to package directions

Salt and freshly ground black pepper to taste

1/2 pound ziti

1/2 cup finely chopped flat-leaf parsley

Stained juice of half a lemon

1/3 cup grated smoked metsovone cheese (optional)*

Yield: 4 servings

*Metsovone (see page 12) is available at most Greek food shops in major metropolitan areas.

Rebecca Aaron, who runs a linens shop in Corfutown, introduced me to some of the traditional dishes of the island's much diminished Jewish community. Some of the Jews in Corfu emigrated to the island from Italy, and this dish seems to evince a certain Italian origin. Pasta and beans are not a common combination anywhere else in Greece. The dish falls somewhere between soup and stew, slushy and warm, the kind of meal you are inclined to slurp pleasurably. It should be served warm, else the pasta and beans absorb all liquid in the pot.

1. Heat olive oil in a large stewing pot or casserole and cook onion for 2 to 3 minutes, until it begins to wilt. Add celery and garlic and continue to cook for 7 to 8 more minutes, stirring frequently with a wooden spoon, until soft.

2. Add beans to the pot and toss to combine. Add enough water to the pot to cover the beans by 1 inch. Cover and bring to a boil over medium heat. Reduce heat and simmer, covered, for 1 1/4 to 1 1/2 hours, until the beans are very tender. Keep adding enough water to keep the beans constantly covered, overall 5 to 7 cups.

3. Making sure there is ample water in the pot, raise heat slightly, add salt, and then add the pasta. Simmer for another 10 minutes, or until the pasta is tender. Before removing from heat, add the parsley and adjust the seasoning to taste with salt, pepper, and lemon juice.

Serve hot, topped with grated metsovone or with grated smoked provolone.

RIGATONI WITH YOUNG BROAD BEANS AND PEPPERY FETA

Makaronia me Freska Koukia kai Kopanisti

3 pounds fresh broad beans, cleaned and shelled (about 3 cups)*

5 plum tomatoes, peeled and coarsely chopped (about 1 1/2 cups)

2 to 3 garlic cloves, peeled and minced

2 tablespoons finely chopped fresh mint

1/4 cup plus 2 tablespoons extra-virgin olive oil

Salt and freshly ground black pepper

1 pound rigatoni

1/2 cup kopanisti (see page 31)

This pasta and bean dish is fresh and sharp with fava beans and pungent cheese, and speaks of spring in Greece. Fava beans, tomatoes, and pasta are a sating combination. Add to it the powerful kopanisti *(peppery feta cheese dip), and watch even the most dubious dinner companions dig in with gusto.*

1. Bring a medium-sized pot of water to a rolling boil and blanch the broad beans for about 7 minutes, until tender but firm. Remove, rinse, and drain.

2. Combine the beans with the tomatoes, garlic, mint, 1/4 cup olive oil, salt, and pepper and let sit for 1 hour so that the flavors meld.

3. Boil the pasta in salted water until al dente, drain, and toss with remaining olive oil. Divide the pasta among serving bowls, top with the broad bean and tomato mixture, and dollop with 2 or 3 teaspoons of the kopanisti. Serve hot.

Yield: 4 to 6 servings

*If fresh broad beans are unavailable, use frozen. Thaw, then blanch and toss as for fresh.

TAGLIATELLE WITH OLIVES, TOMATOES, CAPERS, AND OUZO

Makaronia me Elies, Tomates, Kapari kai Ouzo

5 tablespoons extra-virgin olive oil

1 large red onion, peeled and finely chopped

3 garlic cloves, peeled and finely chopped

1 small chili pepper, seeded and chopped (optional)

2 cups chopped plum tomatoes (canned are fine)

1 tablespoon small pickled capers, rinsed and drained

1 cup rinsed, pitted, and coarsely chopped kalamata olives

2 tablespoons ouzo

1 teaspoon oregano

Salt and freshly ground black pepper to taste

1 pound tagliatelle or other long, flat pasta

1. Heat 3 tablespoons of olive oil in a large skillet and cook the onion over medium heat, stirring, for 7 to 8 minutes. Add the garlic and chili pepper and cook for another 2 minutes. Pour in the tomatoes, lower the heat, and let the sauce simmer for 10 to 12 minutes. Add the capers and olives and continue to cook for another 5 minutes. About a minute before removing from heat, add the ouzo and oregano. Season to taste with salt and pepper.

2. While the sauce is simmering, bring a large pot of salted water to a rolling boil and cook the pasta until al dente. Drain, rinse in a colander under cold water, and toss with 2 more tablespoons of olive oil. Serve immediately, topped with the sauce.

Yield: 4 servings

EGG NOODLES WITH WARM TAHINI-YOGURT SAUCE

Hilopittes me Tahini kai Yiaourti

3 tablespoons tahini

Strained juice of 1 lemon

1 cup water

2 garlic cloves, peeled and minced

1 cup drained Greek yogurt (see page 17)

Several drops of commercial hot-pepper sauce

1 pound Greek *hilopittes* or other egg noodles

Salt and freshly ground black pepper to taste

2 to 3 tablespoons extra-virgin olive oil

1/4 cup finely chopped fresh flat-leaf parsley

1. Beat together the tahini, lemon juice, and water until smooth and creamy. Place the mixture in the food processor, add the garlic, yogurt, and hot-pepper sauce and pulse until creamy and frothy.

2. Meanwhile, boil the noodles in ample salted water until tender. Drain and reserve 1/4 to 1/2 cup of the liquid. Toss the noodles with olive oil.

3. Add the pasta liquid to the tahini-yogurt mixture, place in a small saucepan, and heat for 2 to 4 minutes, just to warm through. Season with pepper, pour over the pasta, and combine, together with chopped parsley. Serve immediately.

Yield: 4 servings

KASSOS PASTA WITH YOGURT

Makaronia tis Kassou

6 tablespoons butter

3 medium-sized yellow onions, finely chopped (about 3 cups)

1 pound penne

2 cups drained Greek yogurt, preferably sheep's milk (see page 17)

Salt and freshly ground black pepper to taste

Yield: 4 to 6 servings

Throughout the islands of the southern Aegean, but especially in Crete and in Kassos, there are many rich cheese, butter, and pasta dishes. One of the traditional preparations in this part of Greece is something called staka, a by-product of homemade sheep's milk butter. It is strong and pungent, an acquired taste for most, and difficult to find outside rural communities. For islanders living in Athens and other cities, however, staka is replaced with thick strained yogurt. This is a very simple but satisfying dish, sweet with onions but tempered by the tart, puckish flavor of the yogurt.

1. Heat 4 tablespoons of the butter in a large skillet and add the onions. Cook over medium-low heat until the onions turn golden and soft, 15 to 20 minutes. Stir the onions frequently while they cook.

2. Bring a large pot of salted water to a rolling boil and cook the pasta until al dente.

3. Drain the pasta, reserving 2 cups of its liquid. Toss with remaining butter, onions, strained yogurt, and enough of the cooking liquid to make a creamy slurpy sauce. Serve immediately, seasoned liberally with black pepper.

SPINACH-CHEESE LASAGNE

Lasagnia me Spanaki kai Tiri

2 tablespoons unsalted butter

2 tablespoons all-purpose flour

2 cups milk, heated

Salt, pepper, and a dash of nutmeg

1 pound lasagne noodles

5 to 7 tablespoons extra-virgin olive oil

2 large red onions, peeled and finely chopped (about 2 cups)

2 celery ribs, finely chopped

2 packages (10 ounces each) frozen chopped spinach, thawed, steamed, drained, and squeezed dry

1 cup chopped fresh dill

1/2 cup chopped fresh mint

1 1/4 pounds Greek anthotiro or ricotta cheese

1 cup grated kefalotiri or parmesan cheese

2 eggs, slightly beaten

Salt and freshly ground black pepper to taste

1 teaspoon freshly grated nutmeg

1. For the béchamel, heat the butter in a medium-sized saucepan over low heat. As soon as it begins to sizzle, add the flour and stir the flour for 5 minutes. Slowly add the milk, whisking all the while, until smooth and thick, 5 to 7 minutes. Cover the béchamel with a kitchen towel and set aside until ready to use.

2. Bring a large pot of salted water to a rolling boil and cook lasagne noodles until firm, about 8 minutes. Remove, drain, and place in a large bowl of cold water until ready to use.

3. Heat 3 tablespoons of the olive oil in a medium-sized skillet. Add the onion and celery, cover the skillet, and cook over low heat until soft, about 10 minutes. Combine the spinach, onions and celery, dill, mint, anthotiro, and 1/2 cup of the grated cheese in a large bowl. Mix in the eggs, season with salt, pepper, and nutmeg, and toss with 2 to 4 more tablespoons of olive oil.

4. Preheat oven to 350°F. Lightly oil a large shallow baking dish (approximately 10 x 14 inches). Spread 2 to 3 tablespoons béchamel on the bottom. Remove the lasagne noodles from the water one at a time and blot dry with a paper towel. Arrange one third of the noodles in a single layer over the béchamel. Spread half the filling over the lasagne. Repeat with remaining lasagne and filling, ending with a final layer of noodles. Spread the béchamel evenly over the noodles and sprinkle with the remaining grated cheese. Bake for 45 to 50 minutes, until top is golden brown. Remove, let stand for 30 minutes, and serve.

Yield: 8 to 10 servings

*Rigatoni with
Young Broad Beans
and Peppery Feta (page 80)*

Orzo and Wild Rice Pilaf with Leeks, Raisins, and Walnuts (page 86)

*Classic Greek Bean
Soup (page 97)*

*Tomato-and-Rice
Soup Avgolemono
(page 101)*

CREAMY ORZO CASSEROLE WITH VEGETABLES

Yuvetsi Yia Hortofagous

2 cup plus 2 tablespoons extra-virgin olive oil

2 large red onions, coarsely chopped

1/2 teaspoon ground cinnamon

4 to 5 large carrots, peeled and diced (about 2 cups)

1 pound orzo

3 cups peeled, seeded, and chopped plum tomatoes (canned are fine)

2 bay leaves

2 to 3 sprigs fresh oregano

Salt and freshly ground black pepper to taste

1 1/2 pounds (about 3 medium-sized) zucchini, washed and cut into 1-inch cubes

2 garlic cloves

2 tablespoons balsamic vinegar

Grated cheese for garnish, if desired

Yield: 6 to 8 servings

The word yuvetsi *literally refers to a round earthenware dish, but the term has become synonymous with oven-baked stews that combine orzo, tomatoes, and any number of other main ingredients. Traditionally, lamb or chicken are roasted with orzo. Here, zucchini and carrots replace the meat.*

1. Heat 2 tablespoons of the olive oil in a large heavy skillet. Add the onions and cook, uncovered and stirring, over low heat for 10 minutes. Add the cinnamon, stir, and continue to cook for another 4 to 5 minutes. The onions should be tender and slightly caramelized. Remove and wipe the skillet clean. Heat 2 more tablespoons of olive oil and cook the carrots, uncovered and over low heat, stirring occasionally, until tender but al dente, about 15 minutes.

2. Preheat oven to 375°F. In a large pot, bring 5 cups of salted water to a rolling boil and add orzo. As soon as the water begins to boil again, remove the pot from the heat and pour contents into a large ovenproof casserole or earthenware dish. Add the onions, carrots, tomatoes, 2 tablespoons of olive oil, bay leaves, oregano sprigs, salt, and pepper and toss to combine. Cover and bake for 20 to 25 minutes, stirring up the mixture every 7 to 10 minutes to keep the orzo from sticking to the bottom of the dish.

3. Meanwhile, heat 2 more tablespoons of olive oil in the skillet and cook the zucchini until tender but firm, about 8 minutes. Add the garlic and stir for 1 minute. Toss the zucchini and garlic in with the orzo, combining well. Uncover the pan and continue to bake for another 50 minutes to 1 hour, until the orzo is tender. Check the orzo and stir it during baking to prevent it from sticking. You may have to add additional water as well.

4. Just before serving, remove bay leaves and oregano and mix in remaining olive oil and balsamic vinegar. Served hot, sprinkled with grated cheese, if desired.

ORZO AND WILD RICE PILAF WITH LEEKS, RAISINS, AND WALNUTS

Kritharaki me Prassa, Stafithes kai Karythia

3 large leeks

1/2 cup extra-virgin olive oil

1 cup wild rice, rinsed and drained

1 cup orzo

2/3 cup dark seedless raisins

1 cup coarsely chopped shelled walnuts

Salt and freshly ground black pepper to taste

2 to 3 tablespoons balsamic vinegar

Yield: 4 servings

Wild rice is a newcomer to the Greek table. This is a luscious combination, reminiscent of the aromatic stuffings prepared by Greeks from Asia Minor.

1. Preheat oven to 400°F. Trim the stems and tough greens off the leeks. Cut into 1-inch rounds and wash thoroughly, making sure to rinse away any trapped dirt or sand. Pat dry. Place the leeks in a shallow roasting pan, toss with 1/4 cup of the olive oil, and roast for about 30 minutes, turning occasionally, until the leeks are dark and caramelized. Remove and cool.

2. Bring 4 cups of lightly salted water to a boil and add the wild rice. Cover and simmer for about 45 minutes, or until the rice is tender and the grains have split open. Remove from heat and drain in a colander.

3. In a separate pot, bring ample salted water to a rolling boil and cook the orzo until tender, about 10 minutes. Remove and drain in a colander, running cold water over it. Place in a large serving bowl and toss with remaining 1/4 cup of olive oil.

4. Toss the orzo with the wild rice and leeks. Add raisins and walnuts. Season to taste with salt and balsamic vinegar. Add 1 or 2 tablespoons more olive oil if the dish seems too dry. Serve either warm or at room temperature.

BULGUR AND CHICK-PEA PILAF

Pligouropilafo me Revithia

1/2 cup bulgur wheat
(cracked wheat)

1 cup warm water

1/2 cup dried chick-peas,
soaked according to package
directions, or 1 cup canned
chick-peas, rinsed and
drained

1 bay leaf

1/3 cup extra-virgin olive oil

1 onion, peeled and finely
chopped

2 garlic cloves, peeled and
minced

2 tablespoons chopped fresh
mint

Salt to taste

Strained juice of half a
lemon

Yield: 4 servings

Another classic among the Greeks of Asia Minor.

1. Place the bulgur in a bowl and pour the water over it. Cover with a cloth and let stand until all the water is absorbed, about 2 hours. (You can do this in the morning and leave the bulgur at room temperature, for use later.) *

2. Place the dried chick-peas and bay leaf in a pot with ample water to cover them by 2 inches and bring to a boil. Reduce heat and simmer, uncovered, until tender, about 1 hour.

3. Heat 2 tablespoons of olive oil in a skillet and sauté the onion until soft, 6 to 7 minutes.

4. In a medium-sized serving bowl, combine the bulgur, chick-peas, onion, garlic, and mint. Add the remaining olive oil. Season to taste with salt and lemon juice and serve, either warm or at room temperature.

* You can also cook the bulgur according to package directions, with boiling water. Whatever method you choose, the ratio of water to bulgur should always be 2:1.

BULGUR WITH FRIED EGGPLANT AND HERBS

Politiko Pligouri me Melitzanes

2/3 cup bulgur wheat
(cracked wheat)

1 1/3 cups water

1 large eggplant, or 2 small
ones (about 1 pound total)

Salt

1/3 to 1/2 cup olive oil

2 garlic cloves, peeled and
finely chopped

1/2 cup finely chopped dill

1/4 cup chopped fresh mint
leaves

1 to 2 tablespoons strained
fresh lemon juice

Salt to taste

Yield: 4 servings

This is a favorite recipe among the Greeks of Poli. I learned about it from Soula Bozi, whose book on the cooking of the Greeks of Constantinople was published in Greece a few years ago.

1. Place the bulgur in a medium-sized bowl and add the water. Toss it a little and let it sit, covered with a cloth, for 2 to 3 hours, until all the water is absorbed. (You can hasten this process by following package directions and adding boiling water to the bulgur instead. Whatever method you choose, the ratio of water to bulgur should always be 2:1, to ensure that the grain stays toothsome and fluffy.)

2. Wash and pat dry the eggplant. Trim the stem and bottom. Cut the eggplant in half lengthwise, and cut each half into four or five strips. Cut each strip into small cubes, a little less than an inch square. Place them in a colander, sprinkle with 1 to 2 teaspoons salt. Place a weight (such as a pot cover) over the eggplant and let drain for 30 minutes. Rinse and drain well, squeezing to remove excess liquid, and pat dry.

3. Heat half the oil in a large skillet and add the diced eggplant (you may have to do this in two batches). Stir-fry the eggplant continuously until it is coated with the oil and begins to soften. Add the garlic and continue to fry until the eggplant is very soft, 8 to 10 minutes. Remove from heat and toss together with the bulgur.

4. Add the dill and mint to the bulgur salad and toss to combine. Season with lemon juice and salt and serve.

PUMPKIN AND TOMATO PILAF

Tabouropilafo

1/3 cup plus 3 tablespoons extra-virgin olive oil

2 large red onions, peeled and coarsely chopped (2 to 2 1/2 cups)

2 to 2 1/2 pounds sweet cooking pumpkin, peeled, deseeded, and cut into 1-inch cubes (about 6 cups)

1 cup long-grain rice

1 1/2 cups peeled and chopped plum tomatoes

1 1/2 cups water

Salt and freshly ground black pepper to taste

Pumpkins, taboura *or* kolokitha *in Greek, are a common sight all over the country in the early fall. In the north, pumpkin appears mostly in sweet pies, but in the eastern Aegean it is used in soups, stews, and pilafs. This particular dish is inspired by an old recipe from the island of Ikaria.*

1. Heat 1/3 cup olive oil in a casserole or stewing pot. Add the onions and cook over medium heat for 7 to 8 minutes, until wilted. Add the pumpkin, stir to coat with oil, and cook, covered, for about 25 minutes, until soft.

2. Stir in the rice. Add the tomatoes, 1 cup of water, salt, and pepper. Bring to a boil, lower heat, and simmer, uncovered, for 10 to 12 minutes, stirring occasionally. Add the remaining water and continue simmering for another 10 minutes or so, until the mixture is creamy and the rice soft. Cover with a cloth and let stand to cool slightly. Add 2 to 3 tablespoons of extra-virgin olive oil and toss just before serving. Serve warm or at room temperature.

Yield: 4 to 6 servings

WARM RICE SALAD WITH GREEN OLIVES AND CILANTRO

Rizosalata me Elies kai Koliantro

1 1/2 cups basmati rice

Salt

2 small bay leaves

1/4 cup extra-virgin olive oil

2 celery ribs, finely chopped

2 large garlic cloves, finely chopped

1 cup large green cracked Greek olives, pitted and sliced

Grated rind of 2 lemons, preferably organic

Strained juice of 1 lemon

1/2 cup chopped fresh cilantro

Freshly grated black pepper to taste

Cilantro, koliantro *to the Greeks, comes to market in the spring. Greeks use it infrequently, preferring instead the seeds. This salad invokes the fresh, crisp, lemony flavors of Greece, even though it calls for a combination of traditional and unusual (for Greeks) ingredients. It may be served warm or at room temperature.*

1. Bring 3 cups salted water to a boil. Add the rice and bay leaves and simmer, partially covered, over low heat until most of the water has been absorbed and the surface of the rice has little holes in it, about 12 minutes. Remove from heat, remove lid, and place a towel over the rice. Let stand for another 20 minutes or so, until all the liquid has been absorbed.

2. Meanwhile, heat 2 tablespoons olive oil in a small skillet and sauté the celery and garlic for about 5 minutes, until the celery is softened but still firm.

3. In a large serving bowl, toss the rice, olives, celery and garlic, lemon rind, lemon juice, cilantro, and remaining olive oil gently with a fork. Season with salt and pepper. Let the salad stand for at least 30 minutes before serving.

Yield: 4 servings

NORTHERN GREEK POLENTA

Katsamaki apo tin Karditsa

1/2 cup olive oil

1 large onion, finely chopped

4 cups water

Salt

1 cup crumbled feta

1 cup fine yellow cornmeal
(for polenta)

1/2 teaspoon cayenne, or
more to taste

Yield: 4 servings

1. Heat 3 tablespoons of the olive oil in a skillet and add the onion. Cover and cook over low heat for 12 to 15 minutes, or until the onion is soft and slightly caramelized. Check occasionally and stir to keep from burning.

2. To make the polenta, bring 4 cups lightly salted water to a simmer. Add the feta and stir with a whisk until the cheese melts, approximately 1 minute. Slowly add the cornmeal in a steady stream, whisking all the while. Keep the heat low. Add the cayenne, and continue to stir briskly with the whisk until the cornmeal is thick and begins to pull away from the sides of the pot, 12 to 15 minutes. Remove from heat, mix in remaining olive oil, and place on a platter or on individual serving plates. Top with the caramelized onions and if desired, additional crumbled feta. Serve immediately.

SOUPS

THE GREEK SOUP KITCHEN

There are no thick pureed vegetable soups in the Greek kitchen, and no cream soups. Instead, there are a handful of elegant and very simple bean soups, such as the classic *fasso-latha*, made with white beans and vegetables, or the spartan chick-pea soup, *revithatha*, which is seasoned with little besides onions and extra-virgin olive oil. One exquisitely simple soup comes from the Ionian and is still the farmer's midday meal of choice during the arduous olive harvest. It is called, aptly, *zoupa*, and it bears a remarkable resemblance to the watered-down wine and bread that was the breakfast of the ancients. Zoupa is made by toasting crusty peasant bread, placing it in a bowl, and drizzling olive oil and warm wine over it. The Mediterranean diet reduced to its absolutes!

Other classics include lentil soups and vegetable soups thickened with *avgolemono*—the egg-and-lemon binder that flavors so many dishes on the Greek table. There are a few unusual, Old World soups, such as the sesame-paste-and-wheat-berry soup of the Pontian Greeks, garlicky yogurt soups, and the flour-thickened nettle soup, an old recipe from Macedonia and one traditionally considered therapeutic. The following recipes are a comfortable—and accessible—mixture of the old and the new.

LENTIL SOUP WITH CHARD OR SPINACH

Fakes me Seskoula y Spanaki

1/2 cup extra-virgin olive oil

1 cup coarsely chopped onion (1 medium-sized onion)

2 large garlic cloves, minced

2 cups large lentils, rinsed and drained

1 cup chopped, peeled tomatoes, with juice

1 pound fresh chard or spinach, trimmed, washed and drained, and finely chopped

6 to 8 cups water

Salt and freshly ground black pepper

1/4 cup sherry vinegar

Greens and lentils both play a major role in the Greek vegetarian diet. This thick and hearty soup is perfect for a cold winter's day.

1. Heat 1/4 cup of the olive oil in a large pot and cook onions, stirring frequently, until wilted, 6 to 8 minutes. Add garlic and stir for 30 seconds. Add lentils and toss to coat.

2. Pour in tomatoes and stir in the chard or spinach. Add 6 cups water, cover, and bring to a boil over medium-high heat. Reduce heat and simmer, covered, for 50 minutes to 1 hour, until lentils are very tender. Add additional water during cooking to thin the soup to desired consistency.

3. Adjust seasoning with salt and pepper. Five minutes before removing soup from heat, add vinegar. Just before serving, stir in remaining olive oil. Serve hot.

Yield: 6 to 8 servings

CLASSIC GREEK BEAN SOUP

Fassolatha

1/3 cup extra-virgin olive oil

3 medium onions, halved and cut into thin slices

1 chili pepper, seeded and chopped

2 celery ribs, trimmed and chopped (with leaves)

2 large carrots, peeled, cut in half lengthwise, and then into 1/4-inch half-moon slices

1/2 pound medium-sized white beans, such as cannellini, soaked overnight or according to package directions

6 cups water

1 large bay leaf

3 plum tomatoes, peeled, seeded, and coarsely chopped

1/3 cup finely chopped flat-leaf parsley

Salt and freshly ground black pepper to taste

3 to 4 tablespoons strained fresh lemon juice or sherry vinegar

1. Heat 3 tablespoons of the olive oil in a large soup pot and sauté the onions and chopped chili pepper over medium-low heat, stirring with a wooden spoon, until the onions begin to caramelize, 10 to 12 minutes. Add the celery and carrots and continue to cook for another 10 to 15 minutes, stirring occasionally.

2. Add the beans to the pot, toss to coat, and pour in the water and the bay leaf. Bring to a boil over high heat, reduce flame, and simmer, partially covered, for 1 1/2 to 2 hours, until the beans are completely soft.

3. About 1 hour after the beans begin to simmer, add the tomatoes. Ten minutes before removing from heat, add the parsley and season with salt and pepper. When the beans are done, pour in the remaining olive oil and lemon juice or vinegar. Serve hot.

Yield: 6 to 8 servings

CHICK~PEA SOUP

Revithatha

1/2 cup extra-virgin olive oil

1 large yellow onion, finely chopped

2 cups dried chick-peas, soaked according to package directions

6 to 8 cups water

2 bay leaves

2 sprigs fresh oregano, marjoram, or rosemary

Salt and pepper, to taste

Strained juice of 1/2 lemon

Yield: 4 to 6 servings

One early June we happened to spend a few days in the picturesque and well-preserved village of Apollonia on the island of Sifnos. I had gotten out of bed early on Sunday morning to go for a walk and to pick up some bread for breakfast. Church was just letting out, and the town's entire populace seemed to be crowded into the bread bakery. Stretched out in neat rows across a mauve and beige tiled floor was clay pot after clay pot, some charred and old, some still the color of soft red earth. They were filled with the island's traditional Sunday meal: chick-peas slowly baked overnight in the village's wood-burning oven. After church, people crowded into the bakery to pick up their pots and rush home to eat their rustic, but delicious lunch. There is something so elegant about the chick-pea—its subtle flavor is at once earthy and refined. Most Greeks, like the islanders from Sifnos, prefer to cook it in the simplest possible way.

1. Heat 3 tablespoons of the olive oil in a large soup pot. Add onion and cook for 5 to 7 minutes, until wilted.

2. Add chick-peas and toss to coat. Pour in 6 cups of water, the bay leaves, and the herb sprigs. Bring to a boil, reduce heat to low, and simmer, covered, for 1 1/2 to 2 hours or until the chick-peas are tender but not starting to disintegrate. Add the remaining water during cooking to keep soup at desired consistency. Add salt, pepper, and lemon juice to taste. Just before serving, drizzle in remaining olive oil. Serve warm.

VEGETABLE SOUP

Hortosoupa

1/2 cup extra-virgin olive oil

2 cups chopped red onion
(about 2 large onions)

3 large carrots, peeled and
chopped

3 celery ribs, trimmed and
chopped

3 medium potatoes, peeled
and diced

1 pound fresh spinach,
washed, trimmed, and
coarsely chopped

1 1/2 cups chopped peeled
plum tomatoes

12 cups water

1 bunch parsley, trimmed
and chopped

Salt to taste

Strained fresh juice of 1
lemon

Freshly ground black pepper
to taste

Grated kefalotiri cheese*

* Kefalotiri cheese (see page
11) is available in gourmet
food shops and in Greek and
Middle Eastern shops across
the country. Replace, if necessary, with grated Parmesan

Yield: 8 to 10 servings

1. In a large soup pot, heat the olive oil and add the onions, carrots, and celery. Cover the pot, lower the heat, and cook the vegetables until wilted, about 8 minutes, checking and stirring so as not to burn.

2. Add the potatoes and toss to coat. Add the spinach and tomatoes and stir. Pour in the water. Cover and bring to a boil, then remove lid, lower heat, and simmer for about 50 minutes, or until all the vegetables are tender. Five minutes before removing from heat, add parsley. Season with salt, lemon juice, and pepper. Ladle into individual soup bowls and spoon a little grated cheese on top.

CHRIS VENERIS'S TOMATO SOUP WITH BULGUR AND YOGURT

Tomatosoupa me Pilgouri

1/2 cup extra-virgin olive oil

1 large onion, finely chopped

4 ripe, medium tomatoes

1 cup bulgur

6 to 8 cups water

Salt and freshly ground black pepper to taste

6 tablespoons drained Greek or Mediterranean yogurt (see page 17)

Yield: 4 to 6 servings

Chris's recipes grace several pages in this book. He has a way with the simple flavors of his native land, Crete.

1. Heat olive oil in a large pot and sauté the onion until wilted.

2. Wash and dry the tomatoes. Hold them from the stem end and grate by hand on a vertical cheese grater (with big holes). Add tomatoes to the onions and simmer for 10 minutes over low heat.

3. Meanwhile, rinse and drain the bulgur in a colander. Add to the pot. Pour in 6 cups of water, bring to a boil, reduce heat and simmer until bulgur is tender, about 15 minutes. Add more water, if necessary, to adjust the density of the soup. Season with salt and pepper and ladle into soup bowls. Add a tablespoon of strained yogurt to each of the bowls and serve.

TOMATO-AND-RICE SOUP AVGOLEMONO

Tomatosoupa Avgolemono

5 to 6 scallions, root end and tough upper greens trimmed and discarded

4 tablespoons olive oil

2 celery ribs, trimmed and cut into thin slices

3 cups peeled, seeded, and chopped plum tomatoes

4 1/2 cups vegetable stock or water

1/2 cup white wine

2 bay leaves

1 small cinnamon stick

1/2 cup basmati rice

1/2 cup finely chopped flat-leaf parsley

Salt and freshly ground black pepper to taste

2 large egg yolks

Strained juice of 1 lemon

The combination of avgolemono and tomatoes is found in the Ionian, whence this soup was inspired.

1. Cut scallions into thin rounds. Heat olive oil in a large pot and cook scallions and celery until soft, stirring frequently, about 8 minutes.

2. Add the tomatoes and vegetable stock or water. Cover and bring to a boil. Add wine, reduce heat, then add bay leaves and cinnamon stick. Simmer, covered, for 45 minutes.

3. Add rice and parsley and simmer for another 20 minutes or so, until the rice is very tender and swollen. Season with salt and pepper and remove bay leaves and cinnamon stick from soup with a slotted spoon.

4. Continue to simmer soup over very low heat. In a medium-sized bowl and using an electric or hand mixer, beat egg yolks until frothy. Whisk lemon juice into beaten egg yolks. Take a ladleful of the piping hot soup and slowly pour it into the egg yolk and lemon mixture in a thin stream, whisking all the while. Repeat with a second ladleful. Turn off the heat and pour the egg yolk mixture into the soup. Stir in quickly and serve soup immediately.

Note: To reheat, place soup in a double boiler. The egg will curdle over direct heat.

Yield: 6 to 8 servings

LEEK AND CELERIAC SOUP WITH BULGUR AND AVGOLEMONO

Prassoselinosoupa me Pligouri kai Avgolemono

3 leeks, washed thoroughly

1/3 cup olive oil

1 celery root, peeled and diced (about 2 cups)

2 large potatoes (about 1 pound total), peeled and diced

12 cups water

Salt and freshly ground black pepper to taste

1/2 cup dry white wine

1/3 cup bulgur (cracked wheat)

2 large eggs

Strained juice of 1 or 2 lemons

Yield: 6 to 8 servings

Celery root and leeks are two gems of the Greek winter garden. Together with avgolemono, they make for a luscious combination that appears in many soups and stews throughout Greece.

1. Trim the leeks, salvaging as much of the tough upper greens as possible. Cut the leeks lengthwise in half, rinse thoroughly, and cut again into thin, crescent-shaped slices. There should be 4 to 5 cups.

2. Heat the olive oil in a large soup pot and add the leeks. Lower the heat, cover the pot, and let the leeks sweat for about 5 minutes. Add the diced celeriac, toss to coat, cover the pot, and let the celeriac and leeks cook together for another 5 minutes.

3. Add the potatoes, toss to coat, and pour in 6 cups of the water. Season with salt and bring the soup to a boil. Reduce heat and simmer, covered, for 35 to 40 minutes, until all the vegetables are very soft. Using a slotted spoon, remove the vegetables to the bowl of a food processor and pulse on and off, in batches if necessary, until pureed. Return to the pot.

4. Add the remaining water and the wine to the soup and bring to a simmer. Add the bulgur and continue to simmer for about 10 minutes. The bulgur will be tender and swollen.

5. Whisk the eggs in a metal bowl until frothy, pour in the juice of 1 lemon, and whisk to combine. Take one or two ladlefuls of the soup and slowly drizzle it into the egg and lemon mixture, whisking all the while, in order to temper the egg. Pour the egg-and-lemon sauce back into the soup. Adjust seasoning with salt and pepper and additional lemon juice, if desired, and serve immediately.

TRAHANA SOUP WITH MUSHROOMS

Trahanosoupa me Manitaria

1/4 cup plus 2 tablespoons olive oil

2 garlic cloves, minced

1 1/2 pounds mushrooms (common field mushrooms or a combination of field and small wild mushrooms work well), trimmed and sliced

2 medium onions, peeled, halved, and sliced thin

1 cup *trahana*

6 cups water

Salt and freshly ground black pepper to taste

Strained juice of 1/2 to 1 lemon

1/3 cup grated kefalo-graviera cheese (optional)

Yield: 6 servings

Trahana brings to mind all the frustrations of childhood. The pebble-sized buttermilk pasta, typically handmade at the end of the summer in rural Greece and kept in cotton sacks for the winter, is the kind of food that mothers relentlessly try to force on their young, and one that, with equal fortitude, children resist. It is an adult's palate, finally, that is required to appreciate this unique and healthful pasta. Trahana is a standard addition to simple winter soups in Greece. Mixing milk and flour to form a dough, which then dries and is milled to granular consistency, was one way for farmers to preserve milk for the winter. Now, trahana is widely available commercially in Greek and Middle Eastern markets across the United States. When cooked, this unusual pasta becomes creamy and thick. This soup is inspired by my friend Takis Petrakos, one of the most creative Greek cooks around.

1. Heat 2 tablespoons of the olive oil in a skillet and sauté the garlic for 1 minute. Add the mushrooms and stir to combine. Cook over a medium flame for about 5 minutes, then cover and continue to cook for another 10 minutes.

2. Meanwhile, heat the remaining olive oil in a large pot. Add the onions and cook over medium heat until wilted but not browned, 7 to 8 minutes. Add the trahana and stir with the onions for several minutes. Pour in the water. Bring to a boil, cover, and simmer for about 15 minutes, or until the soup begins to thicken.

3. Add the mushrooms and all their juices to the pot and continue to cook for another 10 minutes. Season with salt, pepper, and lemon juice and serve hot, topped if desired with grated kefalograviera cheese.

THE GREEK STEWING POT

A friend of mine on the island of Ikaria has an old wrought iron pot that belonged to his mother, hanging as though it were a trophy in his kitchen. Its uniqueness is its portability. It has a square carrying handle, almost like that of an old-fashioned teakettle, with a hook attached so that it can be hung inside a large fireplace or suspended over a campfire. Out of that pot came his most memorable childhood meals—stews of vegetables, grains, beans, and olive oil cooked over an open flame, sometimes in the fireplace, sometimes outdoors.

To this day, the one-pot meal is the backbone of Greek country cooking. The oven is a relatively new appliance in the traditional Greek kitchen; thirty years ago it was more common to take big Sunday roasts or anything else that needed to be baked to the neighborhood or village bread-baker's oven. Of course, most Greek kitchens today are equipped down to the latest microwave, but stew still holds a special place. Greeks like dishes that are well cooked, in which flavors meld together, and in which olive oil is used more as a seasoning than as a fat for sautéing or browning. We like dishes that require bread as a utensil, and nothing fits that bill better than a luscious ragout.

The stew pot is a good mirror of the seasons. In winter, potatoes and olives, beans and greens, mushrooms and onions, and so many other seasonal vegetables are cooked together as the day's main course. One of the unique characteristics of the Greek vegetarian table is its bounty of hearty main-course, vegetable-and-legume, one-pot meals. In spring, artichokes, fresh broad beans, tender lettuce, peas, and fennel fill the pot. In summer, it's green beans, eggplant, okra, and tomatoes.

Most of the stews on the Greek vegetarian table fall into the general category of *lathera*—olive-oil-rich dishes that to this day form the core of the Lenten diet. These are stews and casseroles eaten traditionally during the long periods of fasting that are requisite on the Greek Orthodox calendar. To follow these fasts religiously means abstaining from meat and dairy products for roughly half the year. The stews are filling, surprisingly varied, and unabashed in their use of olive oil, which is usually used as a cooking medium at the start, then trickled in raw once the dish is cooked and just before serving.

Since vegetable stews comprise some of the best-known, tried and true, Greek dishes, I have tried in the following recipes to offer an array of unusual, regional dishes plus a few modern renditions of the classics.

WILD MUSHROOM STEW

Stifado me Agria Manitaria

2 pounds mixed wild mushrooms (1 pound creminis, and 1/4 pound each of morels, chanterelles, and oyster mushrooms)

1/4 cup plus 2 to 3 tablespoons olive oil

2 pounds small stewing onions, peeled and whole

2 large bay leaves, torn slightly

1/2 teaspoon whole black peppercorns

2 tablespoons strong red wine vinegar*

2 tablespoons Mavrodaphne wine*

Salt to taste

1 pound egg noodles or Greek *hilopittes*, cooked (optional)

Yield: 6 servings

*In place of the vinegar and sweet Mavrodaphne wine, you can use 3 tablespoons of balsamic vinegar.

Mushrooms in the Greek kitchen are an ingredient confined to the few knowledgeable souls from damp place to damp place who know to choose the edible ones, when and where they are in season, and how to cook them. I am lucky enough to have two such friends, one who knows Pelion, Greece's most beautiful mountain, and one who knows the pine forests of Ikaria. My supply of chanterelles, morels, puffballs, and other highly esteemed wild mushrooms is secure thanks to them. Both Pelion and Ikaria, it turns out, are mycological paradises, so much so that it's a wonder that no enterprising urban merchant has thought to enlist a few specialists to go foraging in mushroom season.

Greeks by and large are afraid of wild mushrooms, and rightly so, for one mistake can be deadly. Ironically, the countryside brims with dozens of highly desirable, edible, and delicious mushrooms. There are about 175 edible wild mushrooms that grow in Greece. Among them is the Amanita caesaria, *Caesar's mushroom*, which has been considered a delicacy since Roman times; many varieties of Agaricus, including the horse mushroom, A. avarensis, *also delicious and highly prized; the uncommon Prince mushroom, A. augustus; and several wood mushrooms in the Agaricus family, including A. silvaticus and the slightly licorice-tasting A. silvicola.* There are several varieties of oyster mushrooms, morels, chanterelles, and cèpes, as well as even rarer shaggy ink caps (Coprinus comatus), many types of Lactarius—milk caps—including saffron milk caps (L. deliciosus), which Greeks usually put up in brine; peppery milk caps (L. piperatus), which are usually eaten grilled in Greece; and L. volemus. Other esteemed mushrooms include the sweet white parasol mushroom (Lepiota procera); ox tongues (Fisulina hepatica); rooting shanks (Oudemansiella longipes), a delicacy in at least one place in Greece, Arcadia in the Peloponnisos; Jew's ears (Auricularia judea); wood blewitts (Lepista nuda); charcoal burners (Russula cyanoxantha), which, true to their colloquial name, are indeed eaten grilled in Greece; and the mild, nutty R. virescens, one of the few mushrooms traditionally eaten raw. Although I have never encountered Tuber aestivum, the much esteemed summer truffle, my foraging friends and a few Greek mushroom manuals point to Crete as one of its homes.

The recipe that follows comes from my friend Kostas Skyllas, who knows just where to stalk the wild mushrooms in his native Pelion.

1. Clean and trim the mushrooms. Cut the creminis in half.

2. In a large wide pot, heat 1/4 cup of the olive oil and add the onions, tossing to coat. Cover and cook over low heat for 25 to 30 minutes, until the onions are tender, translucent, and caramelized.

3. Add all the mushrooms except the morels, as well as the bay leaves and peppercorns. Toss very gently to combine, cover, and simmer over low heat for another 15 minutes. Add the morels, the vinegar, and the wine. Season with salt and cook for another 5 minutes. Serve hot, on a bed of egg noodles or rice if desired.

POTATOES STEWED WITH KALAMATA OLIVES

Patates Yiahni me Elies

2 1/2 pounds medium-sized potatoes

1/3 cup olive oil

2 garlic cloves, peeled and finely chopped

1 1/2 cups rinsed and pitted kalamata olives (not chopped)

1 1/3 cups (1 small can) plum tomatoes with their juices

1 teaspoon dried oregano

Salt and freshly ground black pepper to taste

Yield: 4 servings

Although it is unusual in Greece to cook with olives, this recipe is inspired from a classic dish from Zákinthos, in the Ionian, where the cuisine is still rife with traces of Venetian cookery. The stew is at once rich from the potatoes, which break down a bit during cooking, and acidic from the brine or vinegar of the olives.

1. Peel and wash the potatoes. Cut them in half lengthwise and cut each half into three or four slices, each about 1/2 inch thick.

2. In a stewing pot or Dutch oven, heat the olive oil over medium-high heat. Add the potatoes and stir to coat. Toss in the garlic and stir. Add the olives and toss everything for 2 to 3 minutes. The olives will break apart a little and the dish will change color and darken. Add the tomatoes and stir. Lower the heat, cover the pot, and simmer the potatoes for 25 to 30 minutes, until they are very tender and the sauce is thick. Add a little water during cooking if it seems as though the potatoes are in danger of burning. Just before removing the pot from the heat, add the oregano and season to taste with salt and pepper. Serve with good bread and feta on the side.

PEAS STEWED WITH ONIONS, FENNEL, AND TOMATOES

Aracas Latheros

1/4 cup plus 2 tablespoons olive oil

2 large onions, finely chopped

4 to 6 scallions, trimmed and sliced into thin rounds

1 large garlic clove, peeled and finely chopped

2 pounds fresh peas, shelled (about 2 1/2 cups)

4 fresh plum tomatoes, peeled, seeded, and chopped

1/3 cup chopped fresh dill

1 medium fennel bulb, quartered and sliced

Salt and freshly ground black pepper to taste

2 teaspoons ouzo

Yield: 4 servings

The spring table in Greece would be barren and lackluster without the classic oil-enriched dish of fresh peas stewed with dill. Greek cooks often add wild fennel to the pot. I opted here for fennel bulb, since the licorice-scented leaves are hard to find in American markets.

1. In a medium-sized sauce pan or large skillet, heat 3 tablespoons of the olive oil over low heat and cook the onions, scallions, fennel and garlic, covered, until wilted and translucent, about 10 minutes.

2. Add peas and toss to coat with oil and to combine with all the onions. Add the tomatoes and enough water just to cover. Cover and simmer over low heat for 30 minutes. Add chopped dill and continue to simmer for another 10 minutes. Season with salt and pepper. Five minutes before removing from heat, finish off with the ouzo. Serve warm or at room temperature.

STEWED GREENS WITH TOMATOES, ONIONS, AND HERBS

Tsigarelli

3 pounds fresh flat-leaf
spinach, Swiss chard, or beet
greens

4 tablespoons olive oil

2 leeks, trimmed, thoroughly
washed, and chopped, or

2 large Spanish onions,
peeled and coarsely chopped

2 garlic cloves, peeled and
crushed

2 teaspoons sweet paprika

1 teaspoon cayenne

1 bunch dill, snipped (about
2/3 cup, packed)

1 bunch wild fennel or mint
leaves, chopped (about 2/3
cup, packed)

1 cup chopped peeled plum
tomatoes (canned is fine)

1 to 2 tablespoons tomato
paste

Salt and freshly ground
black pepper to taste

Yield: 2 to 4 servings

The name is derived from the Greek word tsigarizo, *which means to sauté. This is an old dish from Corfu. In the Greek kitchen, greens are most often boiled and served with olive oil and either lemon juice or vinegar. In several places around the country, though, similarly stewed greens turn up in the local cooking. In Arcadia in the Peloponnisos, for example, wild chervil is stewed. Crete boasts the* yiahnera, *a combination of wild indigenous greens cooked up with tomato. In the variation that follows this recipe, I've also included an obscure dish for stewed purslane and amaranth, which hails from Rhodes.*

1. Cut off the tough stems of the greens and discard. Wash the greens thoroughly in several changes of water and spin dry or drain in a colander. Bring a pot of salted water to a rolling boil and submerge the greens to blanch, for 5 minutes. Remove and drain.

2. Heat 4 tablespoons olive oil in a large skillet and cook the leek or onions over medium-low heat until wilted and lightly browned, about 10 minutes. Add the garlic, paprika, and cayenne and stir for 3 to 4 minutes. Add the greens, dill, fennel or mint, together with the tomatoes. Cover, lower the heat, and simmer for 15 to 20 minutes, until most of the liquid has evaporated. About 3 minutes before removing from heat, add the tomato paste, undiluted, and stir to combine throughout. Season to taste with salt and pepper. Remove and serve immediately with a good piece of crusty bread.

Variation: Similarly stewed greens are prepared throughout Greece, especially in the islands. An interesting dish from Rhodes calls for purslane and amaranth, two greens that are turning up in more and more farmer's markets in the United States and in some supermarkets.

To prepare the dish, have 3 pounds combined of purslane and amaranth trimmed, washed, and torn into large pieces. Cut 2 medium zucchinis into thick round slices. Heat 1/2 cup olive oil over medium heat in a deep skillet and wilt 2 cups of finely chopped onion. Add the greens and squash to the onions and cook, uncovered, over medium heat until most of the liquid has evaporated. While the greens are cooking, wash and trim 2 large tomatoes and grate them, skin and all, on a cheese grater. The tomatoes will be pulpy and liquid, and you will be left with a large piece of skin in your hand. Discard it. Pour the tomatoes into the pot, add 4 to 5 crushed garlic cloves, salt, and pepper, and simmer for another 7 to 8 minutes. Season, if desired, with fresh lemon juice and serve warm.

GREEN BEAN RAGOUT WITH MINT AND SUN-DRIED TOMATOES

Fasolakia Yiahni me Dyosmo kai Liasti Tomata

1 cup sun-dried tomatoes

1/2 cup olive oil

2 large yellow onions, peeled, halved, and sliced thin (about 2 cups)

2 large garlic cloves, crushed, peeled, and minced

2 pounds fresh string beans, trimmed

1 cup peeled, seeded, and chopped plum tomatoes (preferably fresh)

1 cup chopped fresh mint leaves

Salt and freshly ground black pepper to taste

3 to 4 tablespoons red wine vinegar

Green beans—runner beans, string beans, and a host of other beans—are a common sight at farmer's markets all over Greece in the summer. We like them cooked well—tender and melting—even though we eat them at room temperature. The following recipe is a modern rendition of a classic, with one thing borrowed from the island cooking of Chios, Lesvos, and other places where tomatoes are still sun-dried each August.

1. Place the sun-dried tomatoes in a bowl and cover by 1 inch with warm water. Let stand for 1 hour. When ready to use, drain and reserve the liquid.

2. Heat 3 tablespoons of the olive oil in a large casserole or Dutch oven and cook onions over medium-low heat until soft and clear, 10 to 12 minutes. Add garlic and stir for another minute. Add the string beans and toss to coat.

3. Add the fresh and dried tomatoes as well as the reserved liquid to the pot. Cover and bring to a boil. Reduce heat and simmer beans, uncovered, for 1 hour, or until tender. Add the mint and season with salt and pepper. Cover and continue to cook for another 15 minutes. Remove from heat and adjust seasoning to taste with vinegar. Pour in remaining olive oil and serve either warm or at room temperature.

Yield: 4 to 6 servings

TWO ARTICHOKE HEAD STEWS

The artichoke, native to the Mediterranean, has always been part of the Greek table. Ancient writers mention several varieties, including one specifically from Sicily and one that arrived from the shores of North Africa, probably the cardoon, or thistle. Today, artichokes are a staple on the early spring table, around the same time that fresh broad (or fava) beans, with which they are most often paired, come to market. Greece produces about thirty thousand tons a year, mostly in the Peloponnisos, Crete, and parts of Attica. There are several native varieties: the small, wild, thorny artichokes, which are best eaten raw with extra-virgin olive oil, the preferred way in Crete; the Argos variety, which is the run-of-the mill large, green globe artichoke with the compact leaves; and the slightly smaller purple artichoke, which goes by the nickname "Attica Iodine."

Unless one is lucky enough to have a source for tender young artichokes, which should be eaten raw, the preferred way to cook them is stewed, and the preferred stew a mélange of artichokes, broad beans, potatoes, and carrots. I have included that recipe here, as well as an Ionian version of artichoke stew with potatoes and tomatoes, the one ingredient most characteristic of the cooking of the Seven Islands.

ARTICHOKE AND FRESH FAVA BEAN *STEW*

Anginarokoukia

8 artichokes

Cut lemons plus juice of 2 lemons

1 cup extra-virgin olive oil

3 carrots, peeled and cut into 1/2-inch rounds

12 scallions, cut into thin rounds

2 pounds fresh fava beans, shelled

1 bunch fresh dill, finely chopped

1 teaspoon flour

Salt and freshly ground black pepper to taste

Artichokes stewed with broad beans are one of the time-tested classics on the Greek table.

1. Trim the artichokes: Remove the leaves, scrape out the chokes, and leave only the hearts and about an inch of the stems. Have a bowl filled with cold water and the juice of 1 lemon ready. Rub the hearts immediately with a lemon half to keep from discoloring, then drop into the bowl.

2. Heat the olive oil in a large pot and add the carrots. Sauté for 5 minutes, turning to coat. Add the scallions and stir. Place artichokes, stem side up, in one layer over and around the carrots and scallions. Add the fava beans and half the dill. Add enough water to come halfway up the vegetables. Cover, bring to a boil, reduce heat, and simmer for 30 to 40 minutes, or until the artichokes are tender. Add water during cooking if necessary. Remove the lid. Mix the remaining lemon juice with the flour and pour into pot. Season with salt and pepper. Simmer for another 5 minutes and serve, topped with remaining fresh dill.

ARTICHOKES STEWED WITH POTATOES, TOMATOES, AND MINT

Anginares Kokkinistes me Patates, Tomates, kai Dyosmo

2 lemons, halved

8 small artichokes

1/2 cup olive oil

4 garlic cloves, peeled and crushed

1 bunch (8 to 10) scallions, trimmed and cut into thin rounds, including as much of the green as possible

8 to 12 small red potatoes, washed and halved (unpeeled)

1 cup peeled, chopped plum tomatoes (canned is fine)

1 bay leaf

2/3 cup packed, chopped fresh dill

1/2 cup packed, chopped fresh mint leaves

Salt and freshly ground black pepper to taste

Strained fresh juice of 1/2 lemon

1. Squeeze the juice of 1 lemon into a medium-sized bowl filled with water, and have it nearby when you clean the artichokes.

2. Trim the stems off the artichokes, leaving about an inch under the flower. Cut about 1/4 inch off the tops with a serrated knife, and snap off the tough outer leaves, stopping when you get to the white tender leaves further in. Cut the artichokes in half lengthwise and quickly scoop out the chokes. Rub the cleaned artichokes with water and submerge them immediately in the bowl of acidulated water to keep them from blackening.

3. Heat the olive oil in a large stewing pot and sauté the garlic and scallions over medium heat for a few minutes, until soft. Add the artichokes and the potatoes to the pot, toss gently with a wooden spoon to coat with oil, lower the heat, and cover and cook for about 10 minutes, stirring occasionally. Add the tomatoes, bay leaf, and enough water to barely cover the vegetables. Season with salt and simmer, covered, until the vegetables are tender, about 30 minutes. About halfway through cooking, add the herbs. Just before removing from heat, adjust seasoning with salt and pepper and add a little lemon juice, if desired.

CAULIFLOWER WITH ROSEMARY, ONIONS, AND TOMATOES

Kounoupithi Stifado

1/3 cup extra-virgin olive oil

5 medium-sized red onions, peeled and quartered lengthwise

3 garlic cloves, peeled and crushed

1 medium-sized cauliflower (about 1 1/2 pounds) cut into florets

1 1/2 cups peeled, chopped plum tomatoes

1 large bay leaf

1/2 teaspoon black peppercorns

1 sprig fresh rosemary

1 cup water

Salt to taste

1/2 cup dry red wine

1 tablespoon tomato paste

1 to 2 tablespoons sherry or balsamic vinegar

Yield: 4 to 6 servings

Cauliflower is one of those vegetables, even among vegetable-loving Greek cooks, that incites as much ire as praise. The most common way to prepare it is boiled and dressed in lemon and olive oil. This is a simple dish for cauliflower stew. What sets it apart is the rosemary.

1. Heat 3 tablespoons of the olive oil in a medium-sized stewing pot over medium-low heat and cook the onions, stirring occasionally, until translucent and soft, about 12 minutes. Add the garlic and stir for 1 minute.

2. Add the cauliflower florets and toss to coat with oil. Add the tomatoes, bay leaf, peppercorns, and rosemary. Pour in 1/2 cup of the water and season to taste with salt. Bring to a simmer, covered, and let the cauliflower cook slowly over low heat for 25 to 30 minutes. Add the wine and continue to cook for another 10 minutes.

3. Stir in tomato paste and vinegar, adjust seasoning with salt and pepper, and remove pot from heat. Stir in remaining olive oil. Serve warm, with good crusty bread.

*Potatoes Stewed with Kalamata
Olives (page 108)*

Peas Stewed with Onions, Fennel,
and Tomatoes (page 109)

*Giant Beans Baked
with Honey and Dill
(page 124)*

Grilled Vegetarian Souvlaki
(page 128)

BRAISED LETTUCE WITH AVGOLEMONO

Marouli me Avgolemono

2 heads romaine lettuce, trimmed and cut into 1-inch-wide strips

3 tablespoons butter

1 large onion, peeled, halved, and sliced thin

1 stalk fresh garlic, cleaned and trimmed*

1 cup coarsely chopped dill

1 cup dry white wine

2/3 cup pine nuts

1 1/2 cups basmati rice

2 egg yolks

Juice of 1 lemon

Salt and freshly ground black pepper

Yield: 4 servings

*Fresh garlic is a popular vegetable on the springtime menu in Greece. It can be found in many farmer's markets in the United States, but if none is available in your area, substitute 1 garlic clove and 1 shallot in its place.

Lettuce and spring go hand in hand in Greece, and the common garden green is often cooked up in seasonal soups and stews. This is a takeoff on traditional Greek flavors — lettuce combined with dill and lemon.

1. Wash the cut lettuce thoroughly and dry it well in a salad spinner.

2. Heat 2 tablespoons of the butter over moderate heat in a medium-sized casserole dish or Dutch oven and cook the onion and garlic, stirring constantly, until soft, about 5 minutes. Add the lettuce and let it wilt. Stir in the dill and add the wine. Cover, reduce heat, and simmer for 15 to 20 minutes, until the lettuce is very tender. Add a little water, if necessary, so that there will be enough pan juices (about 1 cup) to make the *avgolemono* sauce.

3. As the lettuce is cooking, heat a medium-sized heavy skillet (preferably cast iron) over moderate to low heat and toast the nuts, tossing with a wooden spoon until browned, about 2 minutes. Remove from skillet and put aside until ready to use. In a separate pot, bring 3 cups of salted water to a boil and add the rice. Cook, covered, over medium-low heat until all the water is absorbed and the rice is tender but toothsome, about 10 minutes. Toss immediately with the remaining tablespoon of butter.

4. As soon as the lettuce is cooked, turn off heat. Beat the egg yolks with the lemon juice until frothy. Take a ladleful of pan juices from the lettuce and pour them in a slow stream into the egg-mixture, beating with a fork or wire whisk all the while. Repeat with a second ladleful of liquid. Pour the sauce back into the pot and stir in thoroughly. Season with salt and pepper. Spread the rice on a serving platter and pour the braised lettuce over it. Top with the toasted pine nuts and serve immediately.

Variation: Fresh spinach can be substituted for the lettuce. Use about 1 pound. Trim off the tough stems and shred the leaves as for the lettuce.

CELERIAC AVGOLEMONO

Selinoriza Avgolemono

3 to 4 lemons

1 large or 2 medium celery roots (about 2 pounds, total)

Extra-virgin olive oil

2 garlic cloves, peeled and minced

2 medium carrots, peeled and cut into 1/2-inch rounds

4 medium potatoes, peeled, halved lengthwise, and cut into chunks

Salt and freshly ground black pepper to taste

2 egg yolks

Yield: 6 servings

My friend Roxanni has many talents. She is one of the few women grape-growers and winemakers in Greece, and she has a deft hand with avgolemono. "Celery root needs lots of lemon juice—don't shy away from it," she advised me. The proof of her wisdom is in this tart, tangy recipe.

1. Have a bowl of water mixed with the juice of 1 of the lemons ready. Using a paring knife or vegetable peeler, peel the tough dark skin off the celery roots. Quarter them lengthwise and cut each wedge into 1/2-inch slices. Place in the bowl of acidulated water to keep from browning.

2. Heat 1/3 cup of the olive oil in a stewing pot or Dutch oven and add the celery root pieces. Cover and "steam" in the oil over medium-low heat for 3 to 4 minutes. Add the garlic and toss. Add the carrots and potatoes and gently stir to coat with oil. Pour in enough water just to cover the vegetables. Season with salt and pepper. Cover and bring to a boil over medium heat. Reduce heat and simmer for 35 to 40 minutes, or until all the vegetables are tender.

3. To prepare the avgolemono, beat the egg yolks with a wire whisk until frothy and add the remaining lemon juice. Continue to beat for 2 to 3 minutes. Turn off the heat under the vegetables. Take a ladleful of the pot juices and add it to the egg-and-lemon mixture in a slow, steady stream, whisking all the while. Pour the mixture back into the pot, stir immediately, and serve.

NAVY BEANS STEWED WITH ARUGULA

Fassolakia Yiahni me Roka

1/3 cup olive oil

1 large red onion, peeled and coarsely chopped

2 garlic cloves, peeled and finely chopped

1 cup dried navy beans, soaked according to package directions (once swelled there will be about 2 cups of beans)

2 cups chopped plum tomatoes, with their juice

1 1/4 pounds arugula, trimmed, chopped, washed, and drained

1/4 cup sherry vinegar

Salt to taste

Yield: 4 to 6 servings

Arugula—roka to the Greeks—grows wild all over the countryside. Although most cuisines call for arugula to be eaten raw as a salad, in Greek kitchens it is often cooked, the way all wild greens are. Cooking changes the taste quite dramatically; all the pepperiness of the arugula becomes pleasantly bitter when it is simmered. Greeks like to combine greens and beans in long-cooked dishes. While beans cooked with arugula isn't a dish particular to any region of the country, in spirit the combination is inherently Greek.

1. In a medium-sized stewing pot or casserole, heat the olive oil over medium heat and add the onion. Cook, stirring, until wilted, about 7 minutes. Meanwhile, drain the beans.

2. Add the garlic to the onions and stir for 1 minute. Add the beans and stir around in the pot to coat with oil. Add the tomatoes and arugula and enough water to cover the beans by about 1 inch. Cover, bring to a boil, reduce heat, and simmer for 1 to 1 1/2 hours, until the beans are extremely tender.

3. Remove from heat and adjust seasoning with vinegar and salt. Serve warm or at room temperature.

CRANBERRY BEANS STEWED WITH TOMATOES AND SPICES

Barbounia Yiahni a la Polita

1/2 cup plus 3 tablespoons olive oil

1 large onion, finely chopped (about 1 cup)

3 garlic cloves, peeled and minced

1/2 teaspoon cayenne, or more to taste

1 scant teaspoon ground cinnamon

1 teaspoon paprika

1/2 pound cranberry beans, soaked according to package directions and drained

2 cups crushed tomatoes or chopped fresh plum tomatoes

1 bay leaf

Salt to taste

2 to 3 tablespoons sherry vinegar

1 cup drained Greek yogurt (see page 17)

Yield: 4 servings

I first tried barbounia Yiahni *in Soula Bozi's kitchen. She knows the cuisine of the Poli (Istanbul) Greeks intimately, having spent most of her life in that famed city. The morning I visited her, we were to go to the market together. She turned her electric burner to the lowest temperature, and when we returned after sojourns into fish markets, farmer's markets, taverns, and pastry shops, this thick, rich, spicy bean stew was waiting for us.*

1. Heat 1/2 cup of the olive oil in a medium-sized saucepan over medium heat and cook onion until wilted, about 6 minutes. Add garlic and continue to cook for another 2 to 3 minutes. Add the cayenne, cinnamon, and paprika and stir in with the onions, cooking for another 2 to 3 minutes. Add the beans and toss to coat.

2. Pour in the tomatoes and bay leaf and enough water to cover the beans by about 1 inch. Cover and simmer over low heat for about 1 1/2 hours, until the beans are very tender and just on the verge of breaking apart. Adjust seasoning with salt, additional cayenne, or cinnamon and mix in the vinegar. Just before serving, mix in the remaining olive oil. Serve warm or at room temperature with strained Greek yogurt on the side.

DRIED FAVA BEANS WITH MINT

Koukia Stifado me Dyosmo

1/2 pound dried fava beans, soaked overnight

1/3 cup, plus 3 to 4 table-spoons extra-virgin olive oil

1 large red onion, peeled and chopped

3/4 cup chopped plum tomatoes

2 garlic cloves, peeled and crushed

1 bay leaf

Salt and freshly ground black pepper

1/2 cup chopped fresh mint leaves

3 tablespoons balsamic vinegar

Yield: 4 servings

Fava beans — not to be confused with a dish called fava (page 38) — are cooked a number of ways throughout Greece, but they find their most versatile home in the kitchens of Crete. Cretans love fava beans, and they cook them with potatoes, with tomatoes and cumin, with herbs such as wild fennel and mint, and with plenty of onions. This dish comes from a home cook in Hania, and is worthy of serving to guests, just as she served it to us on one memorable visit.

1. Drain the beans from their soaking liquid, and cut away the black "eye."

2. Bring the fava beans to a boil in a medium-sized pot. Reduce heat and simmer for 10 minutes. Remove and drain in a colander.

3. Heat 2 to 3 tablespoons of the olive oil in a saucepan over low heat and cook the onion, covered, until soft, about 10 minutes. Add the tomatoes and garlic and cook for 2 to 3 minutes. Add the bay leaf and the beans and enough water to cover by 1 inch. Cover the pot, bring to a boil, lower heat, and simmer for about 40 minutes, or until the beans are tender. Season with salt and pepper, add the mint and balsamic vinegar, and continue to cook for another 5 minutes. Remove bay leaf and let beans cool to room temperature before serving. Just before serving, toss with 3 to 4 tablespoons olive oil.

LEGUME AND WHEAT-BERRY STEW FROM CRETE

Sympetherio

1/2 cup dried baby fava beans

1/2 cup dried chick-peas

1/2 cup navy beans

1/2 cup whole wheat berries

1/2 cup large lentils, rinsed

Salt

1/2 cup extra-virgin olive oil, or more, if desired

2 cups chopped scallions (whites and greens)

1 cup finely chopped dill or flat-leaf parsley

Strained juice of 2 large lemons, or more if desired

Yield: 6 to 8 servings

Islanders from Crete can claim two great things to their credit: They eat the most healthful cuisine in all the Mediterranean, and they show no small amount of wit when it comes to naming some of their local, traditional dishes. The name for this one, a mélange of all sorts of beans and whole wheat berries, translates as "in-laws," because, as one Cretan friend explained it, "a lot of different entities have to get on in the same pot!" Sympetherio is a vegetarian's dream dish.

1. Soak the fava beans in ample water overnight. Soak the chick-peas, navy beans, and wheat berries together in a large pot with plenty of water overnight, too. The next day, rinse and drain.

2. Snip off the small black "eye" on the fava beans and discard. Bring the fava beans to a boil in a medium pot of unsalted water. Simmer for 10 minutes, then drain the beans, discarding the water, which will be brown.

3. Place the wheat berries and all the legumes except for the lentils together in a large pot with enough water to cover by 1 1/2 inches. Bring to a boil, reduce heat, and simmer for 30 minutes. Skim the foam off the top of the pot and discard. Add the lentils to the pot, season lightly with salt, and continue to simmer for another 30 minutes.

4. Heat 3 tablespoons of olive oil in a skillet and sauté the scallions for 5 to 7 minutes, until wilted. Mix into the beans and wheat. Add the dill or parsley and lemon juice and continue to simmer a few more minutes, until the herbs are wilted. Remove, adjust seasoning with additional salt and lemon juice if desired, and drizzle in remaining olive oil. Let stand for at least 30 minutes before serving.

CASSEROLES AND OTHER BAKED VEGETABLE DISHES

GIANT BEANS BAKED WITH HONEY AND DILL

Gigantes Sto Fourno me Meli kai Anitho

1 pound dried lima or Greek giant beans, soaked according to package instructions

1/2 cup olive oil

2 medium-sized red onions, peeled and finely chopped

3 cups peeled, seeded, and chopped plum tomatoes

2 cups water

3 tablespoons honey

1 cup loosely packed chopped fresh dill

1/4 cup red wine vinegar

2 tablespoons tomato paste

Salt and freshly ground black pepper to taste

Yield: 6 to 8 servings

Giant beans look like extra-large lima beans. Greeks usually bake them with carrots, peppers, and tomatoes. This recipe was inspired by one I found and loved in a recent Greek-Australian cookbook. The faint sweet-sour fragrance is reminiscent of flavors that Greeks used to like eons ago—the ancients and the Byzantines both had many recipes for dishes cooked with honey and vinegar. The tomato, of course, was unknown then. This is a wonderful dinner entrée, and a great leftover dish.

1. In a large heavy skillet, heat 2 tablespoons of the olive oil over medium heat and cook the onions, stirring frequently, until wilted and lightly caramelized, about 15 minutes.

2. Preheat oven to 375°F. Rinse and drain the soaked beans and place in a large pot with enough water to cover them by 3 inches. Bring to a boil, reduce heat, and simmer, partially covered, for 30 minutes. Remove from heat and drain. Place beans in a large baking pan with 3 tablespoons olive oil, the onions, tomatoes, water, and honey. Mix thoroughly. Cover the pan with aluminum foil and bake for about 1 1/2 hours, or until the beans are tender and the sauce is thick and creamy. Add more water throughout baking, if necessary, to keep the beans from burning. Fifteen minutes before removing from oven, add dill, vinegar, tomato paste, salt, and pepper.

EGGPLANT BAKED IN A SPICY TOMATO SAUCE

Kapakoto

2 medium-large eggplants

Salt

1/3 to 1/2 cup olive oil

2 large onions, peeled, halved, and sliced thin (about 2 1/2 cups)

5 green bell peppers, de-seeded and sliced into thin rings

1 chili pepper, chopped

3 garlic cloves, peeled and chopped

1 1/2 cups chopped plum tomatoes (canned are fine)

2 tablespoons chopped fresh marjoram or oregano leaves

1/3 cup chopped fresh parsley

Yield: 4 servings

This spicy and aromatic eggplant dish is from the region of Vólos and Thessaly.

1. Trim the stems and bottoms off the eggplants. Cut in half lengthwise and then into crescent-shaped slices about 1/4 inch thick. Place in layers in a colander and sprinkle each layer generously with salt. Place a weight (such as a pot cover) over the eggplant and let it drain for 1 hour. Rinse and drain well, squeezing gently to remove excess liquid, and pat dry.

2. Meanwhile, prepare the sauce: Heat 2 tablespoons of the olive oil in a skillet over medium-low heat and cook the onions for about 5 minutes, or until wilted. Add peppers, chili pepper, and garlic, and cook, covered, for another 8 to 10 minutes. Add tomatoes, bring to a simmer, and continue to cook for another 10 minutes. Mix in marjoram and parsley and season with salt to taste.

3. Heat 2 to 3 tablespoons of the olive oil in a large skillet and lightly fry the eggplant for about 2 minutes on each side, until slightly golden and tender. Remove and drain on paper towels. Repeat until all the eggplant slices have been fried, adding more oil as needed.

4. Preheat oven to 350°F. Lightly oil a medium-sized, 2-inch-deep baking dish. Place a layer of eggplant slices on the bottom, trying not to overlap, and spread enough of the sauce over them to cover the surface completely. Repeat with remaining eggplant and sauce until both are used up. Cover loosely with aluminum foil and bake for about 1 hour, until the eggplant is completely tender. Cut into wedges and serve.

EGGPLANT BAKED
WITH WALNUT-GARLIC SAUCE

Melitzanes Sto Fourno me Karydia kai Skordo

3 medium eggplants

Salt

1/2 cup plus 2 tablespoons extra-virgin olive oil

1/2 cup shelled walnuts

2 to 3 garlic cloves, peeled and minced

2 to 3 tablespoons sherry vinegar

1/3 cup water, more if necessary

2 to 3 tablespoons julienned flat-leaf parsley or fresh mint

Yield: 4 to 6 servings

1. Wash the eggplants and trim off the stems and bottoms. Cut into 1/4-inch rounds. Place in layers in a colander and sprinkle each layer with salt. Let the eggplant sit for 1 hour. Rinse and pat dry.

2. Preheat broiler. Brush a jelly-roll pan or baking sheets with olive oil. Spread the eggplant slices in the pan in one layer, and brush the tops with oil. Place the pan 8 inches from the heat and broil the eggplant until lightly browned and soft, turning once, and brushing with additional oil if necessary. Repeat with remaining eggplant.

3. While the eggplant is roasting, make the walnut-garlic sauce: Grind the walnuts in a food processor until they are about the consistency of wheat germ. Add the garlic and process another few seconds to pulverize. Add salt to taste. Add 2 tablespoons of olive oil, vinegar, and water to the sauce, alternating between each and pulsing on and off until the sauce is thick and creamy. It will have a strange mauve color.

4. Preheat oven to 375°F. Lightly oil a 10-inch round pie plate. Starting from the walls of the plate, place the eggplant neatly in a coil or in consecutively smaller circles, overlapping the slices a little. Spread the sauce over the eggplant evenly and bake for 20 minutes, or until the walnut sauce had turned golden brown. Remove, sprinkle with the chopped fresh parsley or mint, and serve.

Variation: This dish is also delicious with either pumpkin or celeriac. For pumpkin, replace the eggplant with 1 1/2 pounds pumpkin, peeled, seeded, and thinly sliced. Saute the pumpkin lightly in olive oil, drain, and continue with steps 3 and 4.

To make this dish with celeriac, you'll need 1 large or 2 medium celeriacs. Peel and trim thoroughly, cut in half lengthwise, then into 1/2-inch slices. Bring a pot of lightly salted water to a boil and blanch the celeriac slices for 3 minutes. Drain in a colander and immediately douse with cold water. Drain, pat dry, and continue with steps 3 and 4.

SPINACH BAKED WITH FETA AND GRAVIERA

Spanaki Psimeno me Tyria

3 pounds fresh spinach, trimmed

5 tablespoons butter

1 1/2 cups fresh dill, chopped

1 pound feta, crumbled

6 eggs

1 tablespoon all-purpose flour

Salt and freshly ground black pepper to taste

1/2 pound graviera cheese, sliced thin

Yield: 4 to 6 main course servings, or 8 to 10 side-dish servings

Spinach comes to market from early winter to late spring in Greece, and this rich dish is clearly a cold-weather invention. It comes from Macedonia, where the winters are long and hard.

1. Preheat oven to 350°F. Chop spinach and wash thoroughly. Heat 2 tablespoons of butter in a large heavy skillet and sauté half the spinach to exude most of its liquid. Repeat with remaining spinach. Drain in a colander and press down so that most of the liquid is forced out.

2. In a large bowl, combine spinach, chopped dill, and feta. Beat the eggs and flour together and mix into spinach. Season with salt and pepper.

3. With remaining tablespoon of butter, grease a 12 x 15 x 3-inch baking pan. Spread spinach mixture evenly in pan. Cover completely with slices of graviera cheese. Bake for about 30 minutes, until cheese is melted and spinach mixture is set. Remove and serve hot.

GRILLED VEGETARIAN SOUVLAKI

Pseftosouvlaki

2 medium-sized zucchinis

2 Japanese eggplants
(usually long, thin, and light
purple in color)

2 large green bell peppers

6 firm plum tomatoes

2 large red onions

1/3 cup plus 2 tablespoons
olive oil

2 tablespoons strong red
wine vinegar*

2 tablespoons sweet red
wine, such as Mavrodaphne
or port*

1 teaspoon thyme

2 large garlic cloves,
crushed, peeled, and minced

Salt and freshly ground
black pepper

8 pita pockets

For the sauce:

1 cup strained Greek yogurt
(see page 16)

1 tablespoon olive oil

2 to 4 garlic cloves, peeled
and minced

Salt, pepper, and hot
paprika

Souvlaki is the carnivore's leitmotif in Greece! I like to drive souvlaki vendors crazy by asking for one with everything except the meat. Here's a home-style version that makes a great lunch or brunch entrée.

1. Wash and dry all the vegetables. Cut the zucchini and eggplants into 1-inch rounds. Slice away and discard the stem end of the peppers. Remove the seeds. Cut the peppers in quarters lengthwise and trim the white pith from their interior. Core the tomatoes, cut in half lengthwise, and gently squeeze out the seeds. Peel the onions, cut in half lengthwise, and cut each half into four wedges.

2. Place all the vegetables in a mixing bowl. In a separate bowl, whisk together 1/3 cup of olive oil, the vinegar, and wine. Add thyme, garlic, and salt to the oil mixture and pour over the vegetables. Season with freshly ground black pepper and let the vegetables marinate for at least 20 minutes before grilling.

3. Preheat the broiler or grill. Slide the vegetables in alternating order onto 8 small wooden skewers. Brush with marinade and grill about 8 inches from the heat source, turning, until the vegetables are tender but al dente and nicely browned. This should take 15 to 20 minutes.

4. Meanwhile, prepare the sauce and the pita: Mix the yogurt with the olive oil, garlic, salt, and pepper and set aside until ready to use. About 10 minutes before the vegetables are grilled, brush each side of the pita bread with remaining olive oil and grill in a dry, hot, nonstick skillet. Remove and keep warm, if possible without burning, in the oven.

5. Remove the vegetables from the heat. Lay one of the skewers atop (not inside) a pita bread, and pull out the skewer. Repeat with remaining skewers and pitas. Dollop each with 2 tablespoons of yogurt and, if desired, a teaspoon or two of the remaining marinade. Sprinkle with paprika. Roll closed and secure, if desired, with aluminum foil, wax paper, or a toothpick. Serve immediately.

Variation: Warm Grilled Vegetable Salad

*In lieu of the vinegar and sweet wine combination, use 2 tablespoons balsamic vinegar.

Yield: 8 servings

Using all the same ingredients save for the yogurt sauce, skewers, and bread, you can make a lovely warm grilled salad. Cut the eggplants and zucchini into 1/4-inch oval slices, cut the rest of the vegetables as for above recipe, marinate in the olive oil and vinegar-wine mixture, and place on a rack under the broiler, 6 to 8 inches from the heat source, until crisp and nicely browned. Toss in a bowl with remaining marinade and serve.

BAKED OKRA WITH TOMATOES, POTATOES, AND BASIL

Bamyies Sto Fourno

1 1/4 pounds fresh okra

5 to 6 tablespoons red wine vinegar

6 tablespoons olive oil

2 large red onions, peeled, halved, and cut into thin slices (about 2 cups)

2 garlic cloves, crushed, peeled, and finely chopped

2 1/2 pounds (about 5) medium-sized potatoes, peeled and cut into 1/2-inch rounds

Salt and freshly ground black pepper to taste

2 teaspoons dried basil

1 1/3 cups peeled, chopped plum tomatoes and their juices (canned is fine)

Yield: 4 to 6 servings

Okra usually is prepared in a thick and hearty stew, eaten at room temperature. This dish is a slight variation. Baking the okra keeps it slightly firmer and lends it a nutty quality lost in the stewing pot. Basil is not a common spice in Greece, but I took license here to add it, since it complements the dish so well.

1. Wash and drain the okra, then trim it, making sure to cut away the tough ring near the stem. Place in a large bowl and toss with 3 tablespoons of the vinegar. Let stand for 1 hour, then drain.

2. Heat 3 tablespoons of the olive oil in a large heavy skillet over medium heat and sauté onions until golden and soft, about 10 minutes. Add garlic and stir for another minute.

3. Lightly oil a large, round earthenware baking dish and preheat oven to 400°F. Coil the potato slices on the bottom of the dish, in one single, slightly overlapping layer. Season with salt, pepper, and basil. Spread the okra over the potatoes and season with salt, pepper, and basil. Strew the onions on top of the okra, pour in the tomatoes, and add enough water to cover the contents by 1 1/2 inches. Cover the baking dish and bake for 1 1/2 hours, or until the okra is soft. Add more water if necessary during cooking to keep the okra and potatoes from burning. When the vegetables are cooked and tender, remove from oven and drizzle in remaining olive oil and vinegar. Let stand for 1 hour before serving.

BAKED VEGETABLE MEDLEY

Briam

1 medium-sized eggplant

1/2 cup plus 2 tablespoons olive oil

2 medium-sized red onions, peeled, halved, and cut into thin rings

2 large garlic cloves, peeled, crushed, and minced

2 pounds potatoes (about 5 medium-large), washed, peeled, and cut into 1/4-inch rounds

2 large zucchini (about 1 pound each), washed, trimmed, and cut into 1/4-inch rounds

2 large green bell peppers, washed, trimmed, seeded, and cut into 1/4-inch rings

Salt and freshly ground black pepper to taste

2 tablespoons chopped fresh marjoram or oregano, or 2 teaspoons dried

1 1/3 cups peeled, chopped, plum tomatoes (1 small can)

Yield: 6 to 8 servings

No Greek vegetarian cookbook would be complete without this recipe. It represents the best of taverna fare and home kitchen fare, and is a general all-round classic in the meatless cuisine of the Greeks.

1. Trim the stem and bottom off the eggplant. Cut in half lengthwise and then into crescent-shaped slices about 1/4 inch thick. Place the eggplant in a colander and sprinkle each layer generously with salt. Place a weight (such as a pot cover) over the eggplant and let it drain for 1 hour. Rinse and drain well, squeezing gently to remove excess liquid, and pat dry.

2. Heat 2 tablespoons of the olive oil in a large skillet over medium heat and sauté the onions and garlic until wilted and clear, abut 10 minutes.

3. Preheat oven to 375°F. Lightly oil a large deep earthenware baking dish. Spread one third of the onions and garlic on the bottom. Place half the potato slices, zucchini slices, eggplant slices, and pepper rings in one overlapping layer on top of the onions. Season with salt, pepper, and marjoram or oregano. Spread another third of the onions over this first layer and top with half the tomatoes. Drizzle 1/4 cup of olive oil over the tomatoes. Repeat with remaining ingredients. Cover the baking dish loosely with aluminum foil and bake for 1 hour and 15 minutes, or until all the vegetables are tender. Remove and cool slightly before serving.

CHARD AND POTATO CASSEROLE

Patates Yiahni me Seskoula

1/2 cup extra-virgin olive oil

2 pounds Swiss chard, trimmed, coarsely chopped, and thoroughly washed and drained

4 large scallions, including greens, chopped

2 large onions, peeled, halved, and sliced thin

2 to 3 garlic cloves, minced

Salt and freshly ground black pepper

8 large potatoes, peeled and cut into 1/4-inch rounds

1 to 2 teaspoons dried oregano

1 cup chopped flat-leaf parsley

1 1/2 cups chopped, peeled, drained plum tomatoes

Yield: 8 servings

Potatoes in a casserole with greens. I make this dish in the winter, when chard is in season and when the cold demands a hearty meal. It can be prepared either as a stove-top stew or as in the following recipe, which I "appropriated" from my friend Dimitri Bliziotis, a catering chef who also happens to be well-versed in the country cooking of Greece. I recommend baking it in a clay pot, which adds another flavor dimension to the vegetables.

1. Heat 2 tablespoons of the olive oil in a large heavy skillet and wilt the chard, in batches, until it is reduced in volume by about half. Remove and drain in a colander. When all the chard is wilted, add 2 more tablespoons olive oil to the skillet and sauté the scallions, onions, and garlic over medium-low heat until soft and translucent. Remove and toss with the greens in a large bowl. Season with salt and pepper.

2. Add 2 to 3 more tablespoons olive oil to the skillet and sauté the potatoes until translucent and lightly golden. Remove.

3. Lightly oil a 10- or 12-inch round by 3-inch deep baking pan, preferably earthenware. Preheat oven to 375°F. Spread a third of the potatoes on the bottom in one layer. Sprinkle with salt, pepper, oregano, and parsley and spoon 1/2 cup of the tomatoes over them. Spread half the Swiss chard mixture on top. Repeat with remaining ingredients, finishing with a layer of potatoes and tomatoes. Press the mixture down a little with a large spoon. Bake, uncovered, for 1 to 1 1/2 hours, until the potatoes are golden and very tender and until most of the liquid from the greens has been absorbed. Remove, cool for 30 minutes or more, and serve.

Stuffed Roasted Red Peppers
(page 134)

Grape Leaves Stuffed with Hummus
(page 146)

Onion Pie with Dill, Raisins, and Nutmeg (page 153)

Greek Olives:
Halkidiki, left,
and Throumba, right
(page 7)

STUFFED VEGETABLES

STUFFED VEGETABLES IN THE GREEK KITCHEN

These might be called the festive plates of the Greek vegetarian. They are a bit more time-consuming than the other recipes in this book, but that is in keeping with the general character of stuffed vegetables. They have always enjoyed the reputation for being at once common and special, the kind of dish one's mother makes on Sunday.

Greeks stuff vegetables with rice and herbs; rice and raisins and pine nuts and herbs; bulgur; trahana; other pastas; and sometimes cheese. The rice used is traditionally a short-grain polished rice, which is softer and stickier than medium- or long-grain rice when it is cooked. Greeks prefer that softness to the more toothsome texture of long-grain rice, in which the grains stay separated and intact during cooking. I have moved away from tradition in the rice-stuffed recipes offered here, mainly because it is difficult to find the short-grain polished rice in the average American supermarket. The dishes below are a mix of what most Greek cooks consider commonplace dishes, such as classic stuffed vegetables and grape leaves, *yialantzi,* as well as more than a few unusual offerings.

STUFFED ROASTED RED PEPPERS

Yemistes Piperies Florinis

12 large firm red bell peppers (approximately 5 pounds)

3 tablespoons olive oil

2 large red onions, coarsely chopped (about 2 cups)

2 large garlic cloves, peeled and chopped

1 cup long-grain rice

1/2 teaspoon cinnamon

1 teaspoon ground cumin

2 cups water

Salt and freshly ground black pepper to taste

2/3 cup dark seedless raisins

1/2 cup pine nuts, lightly toasted

1/2 cup chopped fresh mint leaves

1/2 cup chopped fresh parsley

Yield: 6 to 8 main course servings

Florini peppers are long, red, and sweet, and take their name from the town in Macedonia that they are grown in. Their season is the very end of the summer. I love this dish for the sweet and briny tastes it combines. The filling is typical of the kinds of flavors so liked by Asia Minor Greeks — raisins, nuts, ground meat. The roasted peppers with their sweet-sour and smoky flavor act as a nice foil to the filling.

1. Preheat the broiler. Wash the peppers and blot them dry with a towel. Place the peppers on a sheet pan and broil about 8 inches from the heat source, turning as they blister to roast on all sides. This should take 20 to 25 minutes. Remove and cool.

2. While the peppers are roasting, heat the olive oil in a large skillet over medium-low heat and cook the onions until wilted, about 10 minutes. Add the garlic and stir for a minute. Add the rice, cinnamon, and cumin and toss to combine in the skillet. Pour in the water and season with salt. Cover the skillet, lower heat, and cook the rice until tender but al dente. All the liquid should be absorbed and the surface of the rice pocked. Remove from heat, mix in raisins, nuts, mint, and parsley and adjust seasoning to taste with salt and pepper.

3. When the peppers have cooled slightly, cut off their stems. Peel away their papery skins carefully so as not to tear the underlying flesh, and reserve all their juices. Slit them once vertically and scrape out their seeds with a spoon.

4. Preheat oven to 375°F. Lightly oil an ovenproof glass baking dish. Fill each pepper loosely with several tablespoons of the rice mixture and fold closed. Place side by side in the baking dish, seam side up, and pour the reserved juices over them. Cover the dish loosely with aluminum foil and bake for 30 minutes. Remove, cool slightly, and serve either warm or at room temperature.

TOMATOES STUFFED WITH BULGUR AND HERBS

Tomates Yemistes me Pligouri kai Mirothika

━━

1/2 cup bulgur (cracked wheat)

6 medium-sized firm, ripe tomatoes

1/4 cup olive oil

1 medium-sized onion, peeled and finely chopped (about 1 cup)

1/4 cup chopped fresh flat-leaf parsley

1/4 cup chopped fresh dill

1/4 cup chopped fresh mint

Salt and freshly ground black pepper to taste

Yield: 2 to 3 servings

This is a perfect light summer lunch dish.

1. Place the bulgur in a medium-sized bowl and let it soak, covered and at room temperature, in 1 cup of water for several hours, until the water is completely absorbed. The bulgur will be al dente. (You can also soak the bulgur the quick way, by boiling a cup of water and adding it to the grain. There is a slight difference in the result, though. The quick method softens the bulgur a bit more.)

2. While the bulgur is soaking, use a sharp knife to slice off the tops of the tomatoes approximately an inch below the stem, so that they can be hollowed out easily and their "caps" put back on. Carefully scoop out the pulp and seeds with a teaspoon, being careful not to tear the skins. Save the pulp for making another dish.

3. Heat 2 tablespoons of the olive oil in a small skillet over medium heat and cook the onion until wilted. Mix the bulgur, onion, and herbs together in a bowl. Season with salt and pepper.

4. Preheat oven to 350°F. Spoon several teaspoons of the filling into each tomato. Place in an ovenproof glass or ceramic baking dish. Pour the remaining olive oil over the tomatoes. Place their tops back on. Pour about half an inch of water into the pan and cover loosely with aluminum foil. Bake for about 45 minutes, or until tomatoes are soft. Remove and serve warm or at room temperature.

NOT-SO-CLASSIC STUFFED VEGETABLES

Yemista

6 medium-large firm, ripe tomatoes

6 medium-sized bell peppers

1/2 cup olive oil

3 large onions, finely chopped

1 cup long-grain rice

2 bunches fresh flat-leaf parsley, stems trimmed

4 garlic cloves, crushed and peeled

1/4 cup chopped fresh basil

1/4 cup chopped fresh mint, or 2 tablespoons dried

Salt and freshly ground black pepper

3 to 4 tablespoons plain bread crumbs (optional)

Yield: 8 to 10 servings

Not too long ago, it was common on Sunday mornings all around Athens to see men in their church suits carrying huge round baking pans filled with a mix of stuffed vegetables to the local baker to be baked and picked up after service. Customs have changed, but yemista *are still a favorite on the Sunday table. This recipe differs from the classic in its use of long-grain rice as well as pureed parsley and garlic.*

1. Prepare the tomatoes and peppers for stuffing: Wash and dry. Cut off the stem ends with a sharp knife about an inch or less below the top, so that the vegetables can be hollowed out easily and their "caps" put back on. Remove and discard the pepper seeds. Remove the pulp from the tomatoes, chop thoroughly, and place in a sieve or fine colander to strain. Do not discard the strained juice.

2. Heat 3 tablespoons of the olive oil in a large skillet over low heat and sauté the onions for about 12 minutes, or until soft. Add the rice and stir once or twice. Pour in 1 1/2 cups of water. Let the mixture simmer, uncovered and over low heat, until the water has been absorbed, 5 to 7 minutes. Remove from heat.

3. While the rice is cooking, pulse the parsley and garlic together in a food processor until finely chopped and almost pastelike in consistency. In a large mixing bowl, combine the rice mixture with the parsley and garlic. Add the remaining herbs, 4 more tablespoons of olive oil, the chopped pulp, and the strained tomato juice. Season to taste with salt and pepper. Let the mixture stand for a few minutes.

4. Preheat oven to 375°F. Rub the remaining tablespoon of oil on the bottom of an ovenproof glass or earthenware baking dish large enough to hold the tomatoes and peppers snugly. Stand the vegetables side by side in the pan and fill them with the rice and herb mixture. Place the caps back on the peppers and tomatoes. If desired, sprinkle the tops of the vegetables with the bread crumbs. Pour about half a cup of water in the baking dish. Cover and bake for 30 minutes. Remove cover and continue to bake the stuffed vegetables for another 30 to 40 minutes, until the peppers are wrinkled and browned around the edges and the rice is completely cooked and soft. Remove and cool slightly before serving.

SMALL TOMATOES STUFFED WITH EGGPLANT PUREE

Tomatoules Yemistes me Melitzanosalata

2 1/2 pounds plum or other similarly sized small tomatoes

1 recipe for Politiki Melitzanosalata (see page 40)

2 to 3 tablespoons olive oil

Salt

Yield: 6 servings

The idea for this recipe comes from Lia Dimitrakopoulou, a cook and hotelier in Athens who served this at a winemaker's luncheon several years ago. I loved the idea and took the liberty of borrowing it. It is great buffet food.

1. Using a sharp, serrated knife, cut off the crowns of the tomatoes approximately an inch below the stem, so that they can be hollowed out easily and their "caps" put back on. Carefully scoop out the pulp and seeds with a teaspoon, being careful not to tear the skins. Save the pulp for making another dish. Place the tomatoes upside down on several large plates to drain for 1 hour.

2. Have the eggplant puree ready. Preheat oven to 350°F. Lightly oil a large ovenproof glass baking dish. Lightly salt the insides of the tomatoes. Fill each tomato with the eggplant mixture and top with its cap. Place in a baking dish. When all the tomatoes are filled, cover the dish lightly with aluminum foil and bake for 30 to 35 minutes, until the tomatoes are tender. Remove and serve warm or at room temperature.

ZUCCHINI STUFFED WITH GARLIC AND PEPPER

Kolokithokorfathes Yemistoi me Skordo kai Piperi

2 pounds small zucchini

6 to 7 garlic cloves

Salt

Freshly ground black pepper

1/2 cup olive oil

1 cup chopped, strained, plum tomatoes

1/2 cup finely chopped parsley

Yield: 4 to 6 servings

I had gone to Santorini on the invitation of a friend and restaurateur, Yiorgos Hatziyiannakis, who promised to put me in touch with the island's artisanal cheesemakers and to give a me a general tour of Santorini's kitchen and garden, as well as the opportunity to bask in the most magical sunset in the world. The island's cuisine is a reflection of both its feudal past—there are the dishes of the rich, which include roast beef and puddings—and the cooking, much more interesting to my mind, that evolved out of the poverty and ingenuity of the peasants. Of course, tourism has made everyone rich nowadays on Santorini, but local customs survive intact once you move away from the beaten path. When we went to see one of the village women who still make cheese by hand, we found her in the kitchen cooking this dish for her husband. Outside her simple home was a clothesline strung with small white cheeses draining in muslin beggar's pouches. Inside, the kitchen was redolent of garlic and fresh tomato. This simple dish is an island specialty, but it is not exclusive to Santorini. I have found it in Crete, too.

1. Wash and trim the zucchini. Using a sharp paring knife, make two incisions lengthwise on both sides of each piece, so that the zucchini has two long slits, or pockets.

2. Using either a mortar and pestle or a food processor, mash the garlic together with a little salt and pepper and 2 tablespoons of the olive oil.

3. Preheat oven to 350°F. Take a little of the garlic mixture and stuff it into each of the slits with the tip of the paring knife. Continue until all the zucchini has been stuffed, and place side by side in a shallow ovenproof glass baking dish. Spoon the tomatoes, parsley, and remaining olive oil over the zucchini. Cover and bake for 35 to 45 minutes, or until the zucchini is tender. Remove, cool slightly, and serve warm.

CAPER-AND-CHEESE-STUFFED ZUCCHINI BLOSSOMS

Kolokithokorfathes Yemistoi me Manouri kai Kapari

20 squash blossoms (from about 2 1/2 pounds of small fresh zucchini)

1/2 pound Greek manouri*

3 tablespoons capers, rinsed, drained, and chopped

1/2 teaspoon dried thyme or savory

2 teaspoons ouzo

Salt and freshly ground black pepper

1 pound small, preferably long, young potatoes, scrubbed and washed

4 to 5 peeled plum tomatoes, coarsely chopped

1 teaspoon oregano

1/4 cup olive oil

Strained juice of 1/2 to 1 lemon

Yield: 4 to 6 servings

* Manouri is a buttery, mild sheep's milk cheese and is available in Greek and Middle Eastern food shops throughout America. It may be substituted with ricotta salata.

Where there's squash, there are squash blossoms—at least when one lives in Greece, where there are many recipes for stuffed zucchini blossoms. Sometimes they are filled with rice and herbs, as for classic stuffed vegetables or dolmades, sometimes with bulgur or trahana. This recipe was inspired by a French chef working in Greece. He marries the mild cheese manouri with sour capers. I liked the combination, hence this dish was born.

1. Gently wash and drain the squash flowers. Preheat oven to 350°F.

2. Combine the manouri, capers, thyme or savory, ouzo, salt, and pepper in a mixing bowl. Take a teaspoon of the filling at a time and stuff each blossom. Twist the tips and fold slightly over the middle to secure close.

3. Place the stuffed blossoms in a large, preferably clay, baking dish. Cut the potatoes lengthwise into two or three slices, depending on their size, and wedge them between the stuffed flowers. Strew the tomatoes over the blossoms and potatoes. Season with additional salt and pepper and the oregano. Pour in the olive oil, lemon juice, and 1 cup of water. Cover loosely with aluminum foil and bake until the blossoms are tender and the potatoes are cooked through, 45 to 50 minutes. Check occasionally and add water to keep from burning, if necessary. Taste before serving and adjust seasoning with salt and lemon juice.

CHRISANTHOS KARAMOLENGO'S GOAT-CHEESE-STUFFED ONIONS

Kremmydia Yemista me Tiri

8 medium-sized onions, peeled and whole

1/2 cup soft chèvre

1/4 cup Greek manouri or ricotta salata, crumbled

2 teaspoons dried thyme

Salt and freshly ground black pepper to taste

2 to 3 tablespoons olive oil

Yield: 4 to 8 servings

Late in 1995, Chrisanthos opened a small restaurant in a neighborhood of Athens called Psirri. The area is a little bit like what Soho in New York City used to be twenty years ago—old, industrial, and up and coming. Chrisanthos is one of the most talented chefs in Greece, and at his restaurant Vitrina, he serves creative new Greek cooking. His stuffed onions, garnished with a few perfect bay leaves and some thyme sprigs, are like a post-modern rendition of true Greek country cooking.

1. Using a sharp knife, cut a little bit off the crown of the onion so that the top is flat, which will make it easier to core. Using a grapefruit knife or a potato peeler, carefully scrape out as much of the core of the onion as possible without tearing it. Save the cores for another use.

2. Bring a pot of lightly salted water to a rolling boil and blanch the onions for about 2 minutes, just to soften. Remove, drain, and cool.

3. Combine the cheeses, thyme, and pepper in a bowl and mash with a fork, Adjust seasoning with a little salt. Toss with 1 tablespoon of the olive oil. Preheat the oven to 375°F and, using the remaining olive oil, lightly oil a shallow baking pan large enough to hold the onions.

4. Fill each onion with about 2 tablespoons of the cheese mixture, mounding it slightly over the top. Bake the onions in the upper half of the oven for about 25 minutes, or until the onions are tender and the cheese nicely browned. Remove and serve either hot or at room temperature.

VASSO'S STUFFED EGGPLANTS

Ta Papoutsakia tis Vassos

4 large, long, thin Japanese eggplants

5 to 6 tablespoons olive oil

2 medium-sized onions, finely chopped

1/2 cup finely chopped fresh flat-leaf parsley

1 cup (about 1/8 pound) crumbled feta

2 teaspoons dried oregano

1/2 teaspoon cayenne

Salt to taste

2 teaspoons balsamic vinegar

1 egg, slightly beaten

3 to 4 tablespoons plain bread crumbs

Yield: 4 servings

Probably no vegetable is as revered as the eggplant in Greece and all over the Near East. This recipe comes from the mother of a friend on Ikaria. Here, the eggplants are blanched instead of fried in order to soften them without making the dish heavy or oily.

1. Trim the stems off the eggplants. Cut in half lengthwise. Bring a large pot of salted water to a rolling boil and drop in the eggplant halves. Bring to a boil, reduce heat, and simmer for 10 minutes. Remove the eggplants with a slotted spoon and discard the water. Place the eggplants flesh side up and allow to cool slightly.

2. Using a teaspoon, gently scrape out the eggplant flesh, discarding as many of the seeds as possible. Oil a shallow baking dish and place the shells, hollowed side up, side by side in the dish. Roughly chop the pulp and place in a mixing bowl.

3. Heat 2 tablespoons of the olive oil in a skillet over low heat and sauté the onions until soft and clear, about 8 minutes. Remove and mix with the eggplant pulp. Add the parsley, feta, oregano, cayenne, and salt. Mix thoroughly. Add the balsamic vinegar and the egg and combine well. Add 2 tablespoons of olive oil and mix.

4. Preheat oven to 350°F. Place several tablespoons of filling in each eggplant shell until all the filling is used up. Sprinkle bread crumbs over the top of each filled eggplant. Bake the eggplants uncovered for 50 minutes to 1 hour, until tender and the bread crumbs are golden brown. Check the eggplants about halfway through, and add about 1/2 cup of water if necessary to keep them from burning.

CHRISTOFORO VENERIS'S EGGPLANTS STUFFED WITH ONIONS AND KEFALOTIRI

Melitzanes Yemistes tou Christoforou Veneris

8 medium-sized eggplants (about 1/2 pound each)

1/2 cup olive oil

8 small- to medium-sized onions, peeled and coarsely chopped (about 6 cups)

4 to 6 garlic cloves, chopped

3 large ripe tomatoes (about 2 pounds), cored, peeled, and coarsely chopped

Salt and freshly ground black pepper to taste

1 cup coarsely chopped parsley

1/2 pound Greek kefalotiri, cut into 1-inch cubes, plus 1/2 cup grated

Yield: 6 to 8 servings

Christoforo Veneris used to own Veneto, a restaurant overlooking the old Venetian fortress in Herakleion, Crete. His stuffed eggplants are divine, as though a whole garden overflows from them.

1. Leave the stems on the eggplants. Using a small boning or paring knife, and holding the eggplant horizontally, cut through the skin and scoop away about one third of its flesh from the center, as though cutting away part of its "belly." Discard the flesh, or reserve for some other use. Heat 4 to 6 tablespoons olive oil in a large skillet and sauté the eggplant until lightly browned and wrinkled. Place in a lightly oiled baking pan and season with salt and pepper.

2. Wipe the skillet dry. Heat 2 to 3 more tablespoons olive oil in the skillet and cook the onions for 5 to 6 minutes, until they just start to become transparent. Add the garlic and tomatoes, season with salt and pepper, and simmer, uncovered, for 5 to 8 minutes. Remove from heat, toss in the parsley, and cool slightly. Preheat the oven to 375°F.

3. Place 4 cubes of cheese in the belly of the eggplant and fill each eggplant generously with the onions and tomatoes so that they form a mound over the opening. Sprinkle with a little grated cheese. Bake for about 25 minutes, or until the eggplants are tender and the cheese is melted. Serve warm.

TWO RECIPES FOR *STUFFED GRAPE LEAVES*

Dolmades

Outside my kitchen window, on the neighboring terrace, a grape vine wends its way in and out of a makeshift trellis. I can see it as I cook, and it has become a kind of harbinger of the seasons for me—in summer, it is heavy with fruit; in winter, dry and writhing, a silhouette of its other self. It is in spring, though, that the vine captures my cook's heart. The fruit is still tiny and beadlike, a mere insinuation of what is to come, but the leaves, all waxy and bright, are ready to be picked. Throughout all of May, my neighbor stoops and gropes along the trellis, plucking the tender young leaves for *dolmades*. What she can't savor immediately, she puts up in brine or freezes.

  Dolmades are a year-round food in Greece. Yet despite this dish's close association with the Greek table, the stuffed grape leaf is a culinary chameleon, appearing on the tables of every country in the Near East and changing, sometimes slightly, sometimes dramatically, as it moves from place to place. The whole idea of cooking with leaves is ancient, predating even the use of clay. But in most cases the leaves were simply used as vessels, and not necessarily eaten. The ancient Greeks used fig leaves as cooking vessels, and there is some evidence that they were enamored of the grape leaf, too. Today there are a few recipes where the leaves are used to wrap food that is meant to be grilled, but by and large the grape leaf's sole purpose in the Greek kitchen is to end up as a plump *dolma*. There are several traditional recipes for vegetarian *dolmades*. The best-known, for *dolmades yialantzi*, calls for a surprisingly large number of onions. In some of the Aegean islands, grape leaves are stuffed with lentils and rice, and in the north, pureed broad beans and rice. I give two recipes below, one for the classic *dolmades yialanzti*, and another, inspired by the northern Greek dish, for grape leaves with hummus.

GRAPE LEAVES *STUFFED* WITH RICE, ONIONS, AND HERBS

Dolmades Yialantzi

1 16-ounce jar grape leaves packed in brine

1/2 cup plus 2 tablespoons olive oil

4 large onions, peeled and finely chopped (about 4 cups)

1 cup finely chopped scallions

1 cup long-grain rice

2 garlic cloves, finely chopped

1/3 cup finely chopped mint leaves

1/2 cup finely chopped flat-leaf parsley

1/3 cup finely chopped dill

Salt and freshly ground black pepper to taste

Strained juice of 2 lemons

1 cup plain yogurt (if desired)

Yield: 6 to 8 servings

1. Carefully remove the grape leaves from the jar and rinse very well under cold water. Bring a pot of water to a boil and blanch the grape leaves, in batches, for 4 to 5 minutes. Remove to a colander and rinse with cold water.

2. Heat 3 to 4 tablespoons of the olive oil in a large heavy skillet and add the onions and scallions. Toss to coat with oil. Cover, lower the heat, and steam the onions for 5 to 7 minutes, until wilted. Rinse the rice and drain it as the onions cook. Add the rice to the skillet and stir for 1 to 2 minutes. Add the garlic and stir for another minute or so. Remove from heat and toss in herbs. Season with salt and pepper and toss with 2 more tablespoons of olive oil.

3. Separate any ripped grape leaves from the rest. Rub the bottom of a large casserole or stewing pot with 2 tablespoons of olive oil, and spread a few of the torn leaves across the bottom of the pot, just enough to cover the surface. To expedite the laborious task of rolling up the grape leaves, do it assembly-line style: Place, vein side up, as many leaves as will fit on the kitchen table or counter, snip off the tough stems, and place approximately 1 scant tablespoon (less for the smaller ones) of filling on the bottom center of each leaf. Fold in the sides and roll up from the base, tucking in the sides a little as you go.

4. Place the grape leaves snugly next to one another, seam side down, inside the pan, in several layers if necessary. Drizzle with remaining olive oil, lemon juice, and just enough water to cover. Place a plate inside the pot on top of the grape leaves as a weight to keep them from opening during cooking. Cover the pot with its lid and simmer the grape leaves over low heat for about 40 minutes, until the leaves are tender and the rice is cooked. Remove, cool slightly, and serve, with a bowl of yogurt if desired. (Discard the leaves used to line the bottom of the pot.)

GRAPE LEAVES STUFFED WITH HUMMUS

Dolmades me Humus

For the sauce:

1/3 cup olive oil

1 large red onion, peeled and chopped (about 1 cup)

2 garlic cloves, peeled and chopped

1 28-ounce can chopped plum tomatoes (or 2 1/2 cups peeled, chopped, fresh plum tomatoes)

1 bay leaf

1 small cinnamon stick

1 cup water

Salt and freshly ground black pepper to taste

1. Make the tomato sauce (this may be done a day ahead): Heat the olive oil in a medium-sized saucepan, add the onion and garlic, reduce heat, and cover. Cook over low heat for 6 to 8 minutes, checking once or twice to be sure it doesn't burn. Add the tomatoes, bay leaf, cinnamon, water, salt, and pepper. Bring sauce to a boil, reduce heat, and simmer for 1 hour, covered.

2. For the hummus, whip the tahini, water, and juice of 1 lemon in a food processor. The mixture will be thick like peanut butter. Add the chick-peas, garlic, and spices and pulse on and off until the chick-peas are mealy but not totally pureed. Adjust seasoning with salt and lemon juice. Remove to a mixing bowl and toss with rice and parsley.

3. Separate the ripped grape leaves from the rest. Rub the bottom of a large casserole or stewing pot with 2 tablespoons of olive oil and spread a few of the torn leaves across the bottom of the pot, just enough to cover the surface. To expedite the laborious task of rolling up the grape leaves, do it assembly-line style: Place, vein-side up, as many leaves as will fit on the kitchen table or counter, snip off the tough stems, and place 1 scant tablespoon (less for the smaller ones) of filling on the bottom center of each leaf. Fold in the sides and roll up from the base, tucking in the sides a little as you go.

For the leaves and filling:

2 tablespoons tahini

1/2 cup water

Strained juice of 1 or 2 lemons

3 cups cooked chick-peas (2 small cans, rinsed and drained, are fine)

4 garlic cloves, peeled and chopped fine

1/2 teaspoon cayenne

1/2 teaspoon paprika

1 teaspoon ground cumin

Salt to taste

1/2 cup long-grain rice

1/2 cup chopped flat-leaf parsley

1 16-ounce jar grape leaves in brine, rinsed, blanched, and drained as in preceding recipe

Strained juice of 1 to 2 lemons

1/3 cup olive oil

Water

Yield: 6 to 8 servings

4. Place the grape leaves snugly next to one another; seam side down, inside the pan, in several layers if necessary. Pour tomato sauce over them and place a plate inside the pot on top of the grape leaves as a weight to keep them from opening during cooking. Cover the pot with its lid and bring to a simmer over medium heat. Lower the heat and let the grape leaves simmer slowly for about 50 minutes, or longer, until the leaves are tender and the rice is cooked.

SAVORY PIES AND A FEW EASY BREADS

In the old kitchens of Greece, two tools were part of every home cook's arsenal — a long, thin wooden rod or stick for rolling out phyllo dough, and a large, round wooden surface, a little bit like an enormous Ping-Pong paddle, well-worn and permanently rubbed with flour, on which the phyllo was rolled. These were the tools any housewife could not do without, the tools for making pita, the myriad savory pies found in every region of the country that sustained the family and stretched the larder. These pies offered the way to make a meal out of what was most of the time very little. No dish, in fact, is more quintessentially Greek.

Pita — not to be confused with the Middle Eastern flat bread that goes by the same name — is simply the Greek word for pie. It can be almost anything, savory or sweet, and it is not confined to its classic rendition, that is, a filling baked between sheets of phyllo. There are skillet pies and crustless pies, coiled and S-shaped pies, pies sprinkled with cornmeal, and pies comprised of greens and batter (sometimes made with flour and water, sometimes with cornmeal) that are baked, or made in the skillet like pancakes.

In its simplest form — when poverty and want dictated the table — pita was an easy concoction of phyllo dough (flour, water, salt, and oil) brushed with olive oil and sprinkled with sugar or salt. There are, though, hundreds of regional pies that have evolved over the years out of the flora from place to place.

The region in Greece most widely recognized for its variety of savory pies is Epirus, in the northwestern part of the country. It is a land of rugged mountains and thrashing rivers, rampant with greens and herbs, where, until very modern times, most people busied themselves with the itinerant occupation of raising sheep. As a result, a wealth of cheese pies (sheep's milk cheese) and wild greens pies comes from here, differentiated from village to village not only by the ingredients, but also by the number of phyllo sheets used in a given recipe and even the way they are layered. Cheese pies are likely to be dominated by local feta in Epirus, while greens pies are most often filled with sorrel, nettles, spinach, or leeks. One of the most interesting pies in the whole Greek vegetarian repertory is the Epirote lentil pie, a very old recipe rarely found anymore that was basically a thick lentil soup baked between several sheets of dough. Another unusual pie is the rice, walnut, and raisin pie that is eaten during Lent.

Pies filled with greens and regional cheeses are common throughout all of Greece, but there are a number of unique fillings specific to one or two places alone. In Cephalonia, and elsewhere in the Ionian, savory pies always include rice in the filling. In Ikaria, small, crescent-shaped pies are filled with nothing but wild fennel and onion. In Thessaly and farther to the north, again toward Epirus, milk and pasta pies are common.

The whole art of the pie, though, is less in the filling than in the phyllo itself, a simple mixture of flour, water, salt, and olive oil, sometimes yeast or starter, and oftentimes something acidic like lemon juice or vinegar. The idiom for turning out dough in Greece is to "open" it, and experienced cooks adept at making phyllo are able to open sheet after gossamer sheet from a chunk of dough sometimes not much larger than a golf ball. They wrap it around their dowels and coax it outward with their fingertips, in an act of tremendous grace and speed. The ones with a flair for the dramatic stretch it along the arc of their arm, from shoulder to elbow to hand, and with a quick jerk of the wrist flip it, a perfect circle, into their oiled pans.

The following pies are meant to be easy and light. While all are better with homemade phyllo pastry, they can also be made with the commercial variety. Savory pies are soul-warming fare, and the best-kept secret of the Greek kitchen, traditional or otherwise. It is not without reason that Greeks say about a cook who turns out exquisite pies that she (or he) "embroiders."

HOMEMADE PHYLLO DOUGH

4 to 4 1/2 cups all-purpose flour

1 scant teaspoon salt

1 1/2 to 1 3/4 cups warm water

1/4 cup olive oil

2 tablespoons red wine vinegar or strained fresh lemon juice

Combine 4 cups of the flour and salt in a large mixing bowl and make a well in the center. Add the water, olive oil, and vinegar. Work the flour into the liquid with a fork, until a dough begins to form, then knead it in the bowl, adding a little more flour if necessary, for about 10 minutes. The dough should be silky, pliant, and smooth. Cover and let rest at room temperature for at least 1 hour before using.

Follow directions for making individual savory pies.

Note: The phyllo dough may also be made in an electric mixer with a dough hook.

VILLAGER'S LEEK AND FENNEL PIE

Prasopita

1/2 cup extra-virgin olive oil, plus oil for phyllo

2 large leeks, whites and greens, trimmed, washed, and coarsely chopped

2 medium fennel bulbs, trimmed, halved, and coarsely chopped

1 cup chopped dill

1 cup crumbled feta

1 to 2 eggs

Salt and freshly grated black pepper to taste

Grating of nutmeg

1 recipe for homemade phyllo dough (see page 151)

1. Heat 3 tablespoons of the olive oil in a large skillet and sauté the leeks and fennel together over medium heat until pearly, about 7 minutes.

2. In a large mixing bowl, combine the leeks and fennel with the dill, feta, remaining olive oil, and 1 egg. Mix well. If the mixture seems dry, add the other egg. Season with salt, pepper, and nutmeg and toss again.

3. With 1 teaspoon of olive oil, oil a 9 x 1-inch round baking dish. Preheat oven to 350°F. Divide the dough into four equal balls. Lightly flour a work surface and roll out the first dough ball to a circle slightly larger than the circumference of the pan. Place the phyllo in the pan and oil it with 1 teaspoon of olive oil. Repeat with second dough ball. Spread the filling evenly on top. Roll out the third ball of dough, oil it, place it on top, and repeat with last ball. Pinch the bottom and top phyllo sheets together and roll inward to form the rim of crust. Make two incisions with a sharp paring knife in the top of the dough. Bake for about 1 hour, or until the phyllo is golden. Remove, cool, and serve.

Yield: 6 to 8 servings

ONION PIE WITH DILL, RAISINS, AND NUTMEG

Kremmyдopita

2 tablespoons plus 2 teaspoons olive oil

8 medium-sized onions, peeled and coarsely chopped (about 6 cups)

1 1/2 cups chopped fresh dill (loosely packed)

2 tablespoons dark seedless raisins

2 tablespoons bulgur (cracked wheat)

3 tablespoons grated Parmesan or Greek kefalotiri cheese

1 scant teaspoon grated nutmeg

1 egg, slightly beaten

Salt and freshly ground black pepper to taste

1/2 recipe for homemade phyllo (see page 151)

There are many versions of onion pie, the ultimate peasant dish, throughout Greece. In the north, milk, feta, grated kefalotiri cheese, lots of eggs, and a tiny pasta called trahana are likely to be added to the filling. In some renditions, the pie is nothing more than layer after layer of partially baked phyllo (homemade), strewn with blanched or sautéed onions and olive oil. In the islands, fresh herbs, especially dill and mint, and goat's milk cheese are added to the onion filling.

1. Heat 1 tablespoon of the olive oil in a large heavy skillet and wilt the onions, about 5 minutes. Remove and place in a mixing bowl.

2. Add the dill, raisins, bulgur, grated cheese, nutmeg, and 1 tablespoon of olive oil and mix well. Stir in the egg and season with salt and pepper.

3. Divide the dough in half. Preheat oven to 350°F. Lightly oil a 6 x 9 x 1-inch tart pan (with a removable bottom). Roll out the first dough ball into a rectangle slightly larger than the pan and place it in the pan. Brush with 1/2 teaspoon of olive oil. Spread the filling evenly over the phyllo. Roll out the second dough ball and place on top of the first. Pinch the bottom and top phyllo layers together and roll inward to form a crust around the inner rim of the pan. Make four sharp incisions with a paring knife in the center of the pie and bake for about 1 hour, or until the phyllo is golden and the pie starts to come away from the rim of the pan.

Yield: 4 to 6 servings

SMALL OLIVE PIES

Eliopitakia

2/3 cup extra-virgin olive oil

1 small fennel bulb, trimmed and coarsely chopped

1 large red onion, peeled, halved, and coarsely chopped

2 cups rinsed and pitted kalamata or amphissa olives, coarsely chopped

2 teaspoon dried oregano

1 pound commercial phyllo, thawed and at room temperature

Yield: About 36 pieces

The course texture of the chopped olives makes this almost a mock meat pie—filling and substantial. It is a delicious opener to any meal and a great Mediterranean party dish.

1. Heat 3 tablespoons of the olive oil in a large heavy skillet and sauté the fennel and onion until translucent. Combine the onion-fennel mixture with the olives in a mixing bowl and toss with mint and oregano.

2. Preheat oven to 375°F and lightly grease two cookie sheets.

3. Place the phyllo vertically in front of you and keep covered with a towel. Remove one sheet of phyllo at a time. Cut in half lengthwise to get two strips that are 5 to 6 inches wide. Brush the surface of each with olive oil. Fold each strip in half so that they are each now about 3 inches wide. Brush the surface of each again with olive oil. Place a tablespoon of the filling on the bottom center of each strip and fold up, joining the left corner to the right side to form a triangle. Follow the contours of the triangle and fold up from corner to side until you get to the top of the strip. Place seam side down on the baking sheet. Continue with remaining phyllo and filling until both are used up.

4. Bake for about 15 minutes, or until golden, and serve immediately or at room temperature.

Variation: Make larger but fewer pies by folding 1 sheet of phyllo in half, oiling it, and filling it with 2 tablespoons of filling.

CORFU ZUCCHINI PIE WITH TOMATOES, HOT PEPPER, AND RICE

Kerkireïki Kolokithopita

2 pounds zucchini

6 tablespoons plus 2 teaspoons olive oil

2 large onions, peeled and finely chopped

1/2 cup short-grain rice

1/4 cup peeled and chopped tomatoes, with juice, or 1 tablespoon tomato paste diluted with 1 tablespoon water

1/2 cup chopped fresh mint

1/2 teaspoon cayenne (or more, to taste)

1 teaspoon sweet paprika

1 egg

Salt to taste

1 recipe for homemade phyllo dough (see page 151)

Yield: 8 servings

Corfu, rampant as it is with tourism for half the year, still maintains a glimmer of its culinary traditions. Among them, the widespread use of tomatoes and of red pepper. The first is a legacy of the island's four hundred years of Venetian rule, the second comes from the peasant traditions of Corfu. Black pepper, expensive and exotic, was confined to the kitchens of the rich. But red pepper could be had by anyone who wanted it, as long as you could plant the seeds and wait patiently to grow and dry the plants.

1. Trim the zucchini and grate it, either by hand or in a food processor. Heat 1 to 2 tablespoons olive oil in a large heavy skillet. Add the zucchini (in two batches if necessary) and cook until soft, about 8 minutes. Remove and place in a large bowl.

2. Wipe the skillet clean, add 2 more tablespoons of olive oil, and sauté the onions, stirring constantly, until translucent, 6 to 7 minutes. Mix the onions with the zucchini. Add the rice, tomatoes, mint, cayenne, paprika, and 2 more tablespoons of olive oil and mix with a fork. Slightly beat the egg and combine it with the filling.

3. With 1 teaspoon of olive oil, oil a 9 x 1-inch round baking dish, pie plate, or tart pan. Preheat the oven to 350°F. Divide the dough into two equal balls. Lightly flour a work surface and roll out the first dough ball to a circle slightly larger than the circumference of the pan. Place the phyllo in the pan and oil it with 1 teaspoon of olive oil. Spread the filling evenly atop the phyllo. Roll out the second sheet of phyllo and place it on top of the filling. Pinch the bottom and top phyllo sheets together and roll inward to form the rim of crust. Make two incisions with a sharp paring knife in the top of the dough and bake for about 1 hour, or until the phyllo is golden. Remove, cool, and serve.

IKARIAN ZUCCHINI AND OREGANO PIE

Kolokithoriganopita

3 large zucchini (about 3 pounds), washed, trimmed, and grated

3 large onions, peeled and finely chopped (about 3 cups)

5 to 6 squash blossoms, washed and shredded (if available)

1 cup shredded amaranth or spinach leaves

1/2 cup finely chopped fresh mint leaves

1/2 cup finely chopped flat-leaf parsley

5 to 6 sprigs fresh oregano, leaves only, finely chopped

3/4 pound feta, crumbled

Salt and freshly ground black pepper to taste

2 eggs

1/2 cup olive oil, plus 3 to 4 tablespoons for brushing pan and phyllo

1/2 cup semolina flour

1 recipe for homemade phyllo dough (see page 151)

Like most Greek families, we spend our summers in the ancestral village. Ours is a small mountain village called Raches on the island of Ikaria. Life is slow there, and more so in the summer, when the whole population seems to cultivate a withdrawal from strenuous activity, from the otherwise daily worries of life. Cooking is about the only care one has in August, and even that takes on another pace. Friends bring each other goods from the garden, whence this recipe evolved. It comes from my friend Kyriaki's mother, Vasso, whose garden brims with zucchini and several kinds of amaranth, fresh gargantuan mint, parsley, and—most important—fresh oregano. This is one of the few regional recipes that require using the herb fresh.

1. Place the shredded zucchini in a colander, toss with salt, and let stand for 5 to 6 hours to drain. After it has drained, take a little at a time and squeeze it between the palms of your hand very well, to force out excess moisture. Place the zucchini in a large mixing bowl, and mix in the onions, blossoms, greens, herbs, and feta. Add salt and pepper to taste, mix in the eggs and olive oil, and combine well. Stir in the semolina.

2. Lightly oil a 14- or 16-inch pizza pan. Preheat the oven to 350°F. Divide the phyllo into four equal balls. Roll out the first ball on a lightly floured surface to a circle slightly larger than the pan. Place in the pan, brush with olive oil generously, and roll out and brush the second ball the same way. Place the second phyllo atop the first. Spread the filling evenly atop the phyllo in the pan. Roll out the last two balls, spreading them over the filling and oiling each layer. Pinch together the top and bottom sheets of phyllo, turning them inward around the rim of the pan. Score the pie, first vertically then horizontally, to form serving squares, and bake for about 1 hour, or until the phyllo is golden and the pie cooked. Remove and let stand for at least 30 minutes before cutting.

Yield: 8 to 10 servings

SAVORY PUMPKIN PIE IN A PHYLLO COIL

Samos Striftopita

3 pounds sweet cooking pumpkin, peeled, seeded, and cut into chunks

1/2 to 3/4 cup olive oil

2 medium-sized onions, peeled and finely chopped

1/3 cup crumbled feta

1/4 cup currants

2 teaspoons dried mint

1 egg, slightly beaten

Salt and freshly ground black pepper to taste

3 tablespoons bulgur (cracked wheat)

1 pound commercial phyllo, thawed and at room temperature

Yield: 10 to 12 servings

This is a savory pumpkin pie, and a specialty from the island of Samos in the eastern Aegean, where it is usually made during Carnival. The pie can be baked in a number of ways. It is made with either whole sheets of phyllo or with coiled (strifto) *phyllo, in the pan. Sometimes small strips of phyllo are filled and twisted to look like an S, then set next to one another in the pan and baked.*

1. Place the pumpkin in a large pot with just enough water to cover. Place the lid on the pot, bring to a boil, lower the heat, and simmer until soft, about 20 minutes. Remove to a colander and let the pumpkin stand for 1 hour to drain completely and to cool.

2. Heat 2 tablespoons of the olive oil in a skillet and add the onions. Cook until translucent, about 5 minutes.

3. Place the pumpkin in a large mixing bowl and mash by hand with a potato masher. Mix in the onions, the cheese, the currants and the mint. Add the egg. Season to taste with salt and pepper. Add 2 to 3 tablespoons olive oil and the bulgur.

4. Preheat oven to 375°F. Lightly oil a 12-inch round, nonstick pie pan. Unroll the phyllo and keep it covered with two cloths, the first one dry and the second one, on top of it, damp. Take one sheet of phyllo at a time and place it in front of you horizontally. Brush the phyllo lightly with oil and fold it in half lengthwise, bringing the edge closest to you to the top. Brush the surface with a little more oil. Place about 2 1/2 tablespoons of the filling in a straight line across the phyllo, leaving 1 inch on both sides and on the bottom. Fold in the sides. Fold the bottom of the phyllo over the filling and roll it up carefully, to make a cylinder about an inch in diameter. Place the cylinder, seam side down, against the rim of the pan. Continue folding and filling the phyllo, placing one cylinder next to the other, and working from the outer rim inward, to form a coil. When the whole pan is filled, place the pie in the oven and bake for about 1 hour, or until the phyllo is golden and crisp. Remove and cool before serving. To serve, each person gets a piece of the coil, as if it were a sausage.

CLASSIC SPINACH PIE

Spanakopita

1/2 cup olive oil

2 pounds fresh spinach, trimmed, chopped, and washed

3 medium-large onions, peeled and chopped (about 2 cups)

1 small fennel bulb, chopped (about 1 cup)

1/2 cup chopped dill

1/2 cup chopped flat-leaf parsley

2 eggs, slightly beaten

1 cup crumbled feta

Salt and freshly ground black pepper

Grating of nutmeg

2 tablespoons long-grain rice or bulgur (cracked wheat) (optional)

1 recipe for homemade phyllo dough (see page 151)

Yield: 8 to 10 servings

Spanakopita has become as American as pizza, and is impossible to omit in a book on Greek vegetarian food. What makes this one slightly different from the rest is the fennel bulb, cayenne, and nutmeg.

1. In a large heavy skillet, heat 2 tablespoons of the olive oil and sauté the spinach lightly, just to wilt. Remove with a slotted spoon and drain in a colander. Pour out any liquid left in the skillet and wipe dry. Heat 2 more tablespoons of olive oil and add the chopped onions and fennel. Cook, stirring with a wooden spoon, until wilted, about 7 minutes.

2. Place the spinach, fennel, and onions in a large bowl. Add the dill and parsley and combine. Pour in the eggs and 2 more tablespoons of olive oil and mix well. Add the feta, salt and pepper, nutmeg, and cayenne. If the filling is very wet from the spinach, add 1 or 2 tablespoons of either rice or bulgur.

3. Preheat oven to 350°F. Lightly oil a 12-inch round pie pan. Dust a work surface with flour and divide the phyllo into four equal balls. Roll out the first dough ball to a circle slightly larger than the baking dish, so that 1 inch of phyllo hangs over the side. Brush it with 1 teaspoon of olive oil and repeat with second piece of dough. Spread the filling evenly atop the phyllo. Roll out the third dough ball, lay it over the filling, oil it, and repeat with last piece of dough. Pinch the bottom and top edges together, tucking the pinched rim under the pie, so that the surface is almost flat. The dough along the perimeter will obviously be a little thicker than that in the middle of the pie. Push it outward toward the wall of the dish with your fingertips to form the crust.* Bake for 50 minutes, or more, until phyllo is golden.

Variation: Omit the cayenne and substitute 2 to 3 tablespoons of dark seedless raisins to the spanakopita filling.

*This technique for folding the crust is a little different, and somewhat neater, than the technique of pinching the two layers of phyllo together and simply rolling the edge inward to form the rim of dough around the pie.

NAFSIKA'S CHEESE AND EGG PIE

Tyropita tis Nafsikas

8 jumbo eggs

2 1/2 pounds feta, rinsed, drained, and crumbled

1 teaspoon freshly ground black pepper (or more to taste)

2 tablespoons dried basil

4 tablespoons unsalted butter, melted

1/4 cup olive oil

1 pound commercial phyllo, thawed and at room temperature

Yield: 10 to 12 servings

There are probably as many cheese pie recipes in Greece as there are villages. Every region, almost every home cook, claims one. This comes from a friend who grew up in Agrinio, in the central northwestern part of Greece, a land where tobacco grows high and goats and sheep range unhindered. The cheese is ample in this recipe, one telltale sign that the pie hails from a colder clime.

1. Preheat oven to 350°F. Butter a 14-inch round or square baking pan.

2. Using an electric mixer, beat the eggs until frothy and very yellow. Stir in the crumbled feta, pepper, and basil. The mixture will be loose and liquid.

3. Combine the melted butter and olive oil in a bowl. Spread 6 sheets of phyllo pastry on the bottom of the baking pan, brushing each layer with a little of the butter mixture. Spread about 1 cup of the egg mixture evenly atop the phyllo. Place 1 sheet of phyllo over it, brush with butter, and spread about a ladleful of the egg mixture over it. Repeat with 4 or 5 more sheets of phyllo, until all the filling is used. Top with 6 more sheets of phyllo, brushing each with a little butter and oil. Coat the top sheet with any remaining butter and oil.

4. Using a sharp knife, score the pie into square or diamond-shaped pieces. Bake for 1 to 1 1/2 hours, or until the phyllo is golden and the filling set. Remove and cool slightly before cutting. Serve warm or at room temperature.

WILD GREENS PIE

Hortopita

2 pounds mixed greens (any combination of sorrel, chard, dandelion, and wild fennel)

3/4 cup olive oil, plus more for brushing dough

2 large onions, finely chopped

1 bunch scallions, trimmed and finely chopped

1/2 cup chopped dill

1/2 cup chopped flat-leaf parsley

1/3 cup chopped fresh mint leaves

1 small bunch chervil, tough stems discarded, finely chopped

Salt and freshly ground black pepper

3 to 4 tablespoons semolina, rice, or trahana

1 recipe for homemade phyllo dough (see page 151)

Yield: 8 to 10 servings

In the Greek countryside, any edible weed and herb falls under the heading of wild greens or horta, *including such oddities as poppy leaves and such common ingredients as parsley. Cooks all over Greece blend many different greens to make* hortopita, *and the content of these savory pies often changes with the season. The only rule is to avoid bitter greens—amaranth, which is common in Greece, mustard greens, and leafy greens in the cabbage family such as collards and kale. These greens are never used in pies because they are too strongly flavored. They are boiled instead for salad.*

On the question of cheese in greens pies, the decision is really up to the cook. I prefer wild greens pies without cheese. The flavor seems truer to the good taste of the greens themselves, all cooked together with little seasoning besides salt and olive oil to enhance them. Ditto for eggs. Wild greens pies, as they are made in the Greek countryside, usually lack eggs. Instead, extravagant amounts of olive oil—sometimes more than a cup if the pie is large—keep the filling moist. The texture is different without eggs, granted—a little rougher and not so very compact.

Greek home cooks generally do not sauté greens to reduce their moisture content before they go into a filling. They salt them instead. First, the greens are washed and chopped fine and placed in a large colander, then they are literally kneaded with a little salt and left to drain, usually for several hours or overnight. They are not rinsed afterward but are squeezed thoroughly dry between the palms of the hand. I have not recommended this method here, simply because it takes too long, even though sautéing leaches out some of the nutritional components.

1. Trim the tough stems from the greens, chop or shred them, and wash them thoroughly. Spin them through a salad spinner if possible to ride them of as much water as possible.

2. Heat 2 tablespoons of the olive oil in a large heavy skillet and sauté the greens, tossing frequently, until as much of their moisture as possible has evaporated, 7 to 10 minutes. Remove and place in a large mixing bowl. Heat 1 or 2 more tablespoons of olive oil in the skillet and sauté the onions and scallions oven medium-low heat until wilted and very lightly browned, about 10 minutes. Add them to the greens. Mix in the dill, parsley, mint, and chervil. Season with salt and pepper and add the remaining olive oil. If the filling is very wet, mix in either the semolina, rice, or trahana.

3. Have the phyllo dough ready and divided into four equal balls. Have a large shallow baking dish or a 14-inch pizza pan lightly oiled. Preheat the oven to 350°F.

4. Using a rolling pin, roll out the first dough ball on a lightly floured surface to a circle slightly larger than the pan. Carefully place the dough in the pan and brush its surface with oil. Repeat with second dough ball, brushing the surface with olive oil. Spread the filling evenly atop the phyllo. Roll out the third dough ball, lay it over the filling, oil it, and repeat with last piece of dough. Pinch together the top and bottom sheets of phyllo, turning them inward around the rim of the pan. Take a sharp knife and score the pie from top to bottom, first in equally spaced rows then diagonally to form diamond-shaped pieces. Bake for about 1 hour, or until the dough is deep golden and set. Cool for at least 30 minutes before serving.

Note: Greens pies are traditionally eaten at room temperature in Greece.

CHEESE AND SQUASH PIE

Kritiko Boureki

2 pounds zucchini, trimmed and cut into 1/4-inch rounds

Salt

1/2 pound ricotta

1/2 pound feta, crumbled

1/4 cup plain yogurt

1 recipe for phyllo dough (see page 151), or 12 sheets of commercial phyllo, thawed and at room temperature

4 tablespoons olive oil (slightly more if using commercial phyllo)

1/4 cup all-purpose flour

Freshly ground black pepper to taste

2 teaspoons dried mint

Yield: 8 to 10 servings

This dish comes from Hania in Crete. Traditionally it is made with a local cheese called xinomizithra, which is sour like feta but much creamier. The cheese is difficult, if not impossible, to find in America, but a good simulation comes from combining feta, ricotta, and yogurt.

1. Layer the zucchini in a colander, lightly salting each layer. Press the zucchini down in the colander with the cover of a pot and let it drain for 30 minutes. Rinse and pat dry with a lint-free towel.

2. In a medium-sized bowl, stir together the ricotta, feta, and yogurt.

3. Divide the phyllo dough in half.* Oil a 12-inch round pan with 1 tablespoon of olive oil. Preheat oven to 375°F. Lightly dust a work surface with flour and roll out the first ball of dough to a circle slightly larger than the pan. Place the phyllo in the pan and brush with 1 tablespoon of olive oil.

4. Pour 1/4 cup of flour into a dish and toss a handful of the zucchini in it to dredge. Place the zucchini neatly on the bottom of the pan, starting from the rim and working toward the center, overlapping each slice a little, and dredging and adding more zucchini (roughly half of it) until the bottom dough is covered completely. Dot generously with half the cheese mixture, season with pepper, and sprinkle with 1/2 teaspoon of mint. Dredge remaining zucchini, adding a little more flour if necessary, and repeat layering and seasoning.

5. Roll out second dough ball, place over the filling, and neatly pinch together and turn in the edges to form a thick rim. Brush the top with remaining olive oil. Bake for about 50 minutes, or until the pastry is golden. Remove and cool for at least 15 minutes before serving.

*If you are using commercial dough, use 7 sheets on the bottom, brushing each with 1/2 teaspoon of olive oil, and 5 sheets on top, also brushed with oil.

GREEN OLIVE AND RED PEPPER CORN BREAD

Bobota Almiri me Elies kai Kokkines Piperies

1 cup all-purpose flour

1 1/2 cups coarse yellow cornmeal

1 teaspoon salt

2 teaspoons baking powder

1 teaspoon oregano

1/2 teaspoon freshly ground black pepper

1 cup milk, at room temperature

1/4 cup olive oil

1 egg, slightly beaten

1 1/2 cups cracked green olives, pitted and coarsely chopped

1/2 cup coarsely chopped roasted red peppers (about 2 medium-sized peppers)

2 tablespoons seeded, chopped, pickled peperoncini (small pickled green peppers)

1/2 cup crumbled feta

1 tablespoon unsalted butter or olive oil for oiling pan

Cornmeal is not the traditional stuff of breads in Greece, although there are several recipes for sweet and savory corn breads and cakes that come from the northwestern part of the country. This is a new recipe, one that was born in the bread bakeries of Athens.

1. Butter a 12-inch round ovenproof pie plate. Preheat the oven to 375°F.

2. In a large bowl, combine the flour, cornmeal, salt, baking powder, oregano, and pepper. Mix thoroughly and make a well in the center. Add the milk, olive oil, egg, olives, peppers, and feta and mix vigorously with a rubber spatula until a thick batter forms.

3. Pour the batter into the pie plate and bake for 35 to 40 minutes, until the corn bread starts to pull away from the rim of the pan. Remove and cool in the plate. When the bread has cooled, run a dull knife around the inner rim to loosen it. Place a serving plate over the pie plate and flip over the corn bread twice, so that the mounded side is facing up. Serve immediately, or cool completely, wrap in aluminum foil, and refrigerate. Bring refrigerated corn bread to room temperature before serving.

Yield: 6 to 8 servings

CHEESE BREAD

Tyropsomo

1 1/4 cups warm water

1 tablespoon active dry yeast

3 1/2 to 4 cups bread flour

1 teaspoon salt

1/4 pound feta, crumbled

1/4 pound Greek graviera cheese, grated

1/2 teaspoon freshly ground black pepper

1 teaspoon dried mint, oregano, thyme, or dill

2 tablespoons olive oil

Yield: 8 to 10 servings

1. Combine the water and yeast with 2 tablespoons of the flour in a bowl. Cover and let stand for 10 minutes, until the yeast begins to froth. In the bowl of a mixer equipped with a dough hook, place 3 1/2 cups flour and the salt, making a well in the center. Add the water and yeast and mix at medium-low speed with the dough hook until a mass of dough forms.

2. Continue to mix, slightly more vigorously, for about 7 minutes, or until the dough is silky and does not stick. Add remaining flour, if necessary, to achieve this texture. Remove the dough and let it rest, covered and in a warm, draft-free place, for 1 hour.

3. Add the cheeses, pepper, and herbs to the dough and knead by hand on a lightly floured surface until the ingredients are worked into the dough. Divide the dough into three small balls and keep covered for a few minutes. Lightly oil two large baking sheets and preheat the oven to 375°F.

4. Using a rolling pin, roll out each of the balls to a circle about 10 inches in diameter. Place the circles on the baking sheets, cover with a cloth, and let rest for 30 minutes, to rise a second time. Using the tips of your fingers, create an uneven surface on the dough and spread it out a bit more in the pans. The surface should be similar to that of an Italian foccacia. Bake in a hot oven for about 30 minutes, or until the bread is golden. Remove and cool before serving.

EGG DISHES

EGGS IN THE GREEK KITCHEN

At the Central Market in Athens, and at nearly every one of Greece's farmer's markets, there are vendors who sell nothing but eggs, attesting perhaps to their important place on the table and in the kitchen. I find it heartening that even though the Central Market is located in the commercial center of the city, the individual buyer is still accepted, even honored. You can buy just one egg (for about 15 cents) or dozens. They are stacked like towers in cardboard trays.

Without a doubt, the best-known use for eggs in the Greek kitchen is in the *avgolemono*, or egg-and-lemon sauce, which graces vegetables and acts as a thickener for many soups and stews Eggs appear in multitude in many of the holiday breads of Greece as well, and of course hard-boiled, red-dyed eggs are the first food with which Greeks break the Easter fast.

But eggs appear frequently on the everyday table, too. They often make for a casual, quick meal, combined with vegetables or cheese in baked and panfried omelets, frittatas, and other dishes. The recipes here include some of the most familiar on Greek tables as well as a few more obscure dishes, such as the pie-like baked omelet with cornmeal and chestnuts.

EGGS STUFFED WITH CAPERS AND FETA

Avga Yemista me Kapari kai Feta

4 large eggs

1/4 cup crumbled feta

1 tablespoon finely chopped drained capers

2 tablespoon extra-virgin olive oil

1/2 teaspoon oregano

Salt to taste

Cayenne for garnish

Fresh flat-leaf parsley for garnish

1. Place the eggs in a small pan and cover with warm water. Bring to a simmer over medium heat and cook for 12 minutes. Immediately run the eggs under cold water to cool. Drain and peel.

2. While the eggs are cooking, whip together the feta and capers in a food processor or blender.

3. Cut the eggs in half lengthwise and carefully scoop the yolks into a bowl. Using a fork, mash the yolks with 1 tablespoon of the olive oil. Add the feta and caper mixture, the oregano, and the remaining tablespoon of olive oil. Season with salt to taste. Place a little of the filling into each of the whites, mounding it slightly, Sprinkle lightly with cayenne and garnish each stuffed white with a parsley leaf. Serve immediately.

Yield: 4 to 8 servings

BAKED OMELET WITH CHESTNUTS AND FETA

Omeleta me Kastana kai Feta

5 tablespoons olive oil

1 large onion, finely chopped (about 1 cup)

1 cup boiled and peeled chestnuts

2 cups milk (skim is fine)

Salt to taste

1/4 cup finely ground yellow cornmeal

4 eggs, lightly beaten

1 cup crumbled feta

Salt and freshly ground black pepper to taste

Yield: 6 to 8 servings

Nuts and eggs are an unusual combination, but one that exists in several old Greek recipes. This omelet is adapted from a traditional local dish from the island of Chios.

1. Heat 2 tablespoons of the olive oil in a skillet, add the onion, put the lid on the pan, and cook over very low heat for 5 to 6 minutes. Coarsely chop or crumble the chestnuts and combine with the onion. Using 1 tablespoon of olive oil, grease a 10-inch round overproof glass or ceramic baking dish. Preheat oven to 350°F.

2. Heat the milk in a medium-sized saucepan. Before it scalds, add the cornmeal in a steady drizzle, whisking all the while to avoid forming lumps. Lower the heat and continue to whisk until the mixture thickens to the consistency of a loose porridge. This will take only about 5 minutes. Stir in the remaining 2 tablespoons of olive oil.

3. Whisk or beat (at medium speed on electric mixer) the eggs in a medium-sized bowl until frothy, 3 to 4 minutes. Add a little of the hot cornmeal to the eggs, whisking in order to temper them. Pour the eggs into the cornmeal, together with the chestnuts, onion, and crumbled feta. Season with salt and pepper and pour into the oiled baking dish. Bake for about 35 minutes, until omelet is lightly browned on top and set. A toothpick inserted in the center should come out clean, but the omelet should be springy, not dense. Remove, cool slightly, and cut into serving wedges.

BAKED OMELET WITH ZUCCHINI, POTATOES, AND FENNEL

Sfouggato me Kolokithaki, Patates kai Maratho

1 large potato (about 1/2 pound), peeled and whole

1 pound zucchini

1 small fennel bulb with leaves

6 tablespoons olive oil

1 large red onion, peeled and chopped

6 eggs

Salt and freshly ground black pepper to taste

Yield: 6 servings

1. Boil the potato in ample salted water until cooked but firm, about 20 minutes. Remove and cool. While the potato is boiling, trim the ends off the zucchini and grate, either by hand or using the grating wheel of a food processor. Trim the fennel—cut off the stem end and the tough outer layer—and chop the remaining bulb. Discard most of the tough upper green stems, but retain and chop the feathery leaves.

2. Heat 4 tablespoons of the olive oil in a large skillet and sauté the zucchini over medium-high heat, stirring, until most of the liquid has evaporated. Add the onion and chopped fennel (bulb and leaves) and continue to cook for another 8 to 10 minutes over medium heat until the onion and fennel are wilted and lightly browned. While the zucchini and fennel are cooking, grate the boiled potato or pass it through a ricer. Add the potato to the onion and zucchini mixture about 2 minutes before removing from heat.

3. Remove the vegetables to a mixing bowl and let them stand for a few minutes to cool. Oil a 10-inch round ovenproof glass baking dish with the remaining olive oil and preheat the oven to 350°F. Beat the eggs until frothy and pour into the vegetables. Season with salt and pepper. Pour the mixture into the baking dish and bake for about 50 minutes, or until the omelet is set and golden. Remove, let stand for a few minutes, cut into 6 wedges, and serve immediately.

ASPARAGUS FRITTATA

Sparangi Fritata

1 pound fresh asparagus, trimmed

6 eggs

1/2 cup grated kefalotiri or Parmesan cheese

Salt and freshly ground black pepper to taste

4 tablespoons olive oil

Yield: 4 to 6 servings

This dish is traditionally made with wild asparagus, one of the stars of the Greek wild greens repertory. It grows wild in the spring in many places in Greece, but especially in Pelion and in parts of the Peloponnisos. You can find the almost foot-long, thin, and pleasantly bitter shoots at farmer's markets in Athens as well. Unfortunately, wild asparagus is virtually impossible to find in the United States, so I have substituted the sweeter, tamer, ordinary asparagus here.

1. Bring ample salted water to a boil and blanch the asparagus for about 5 minutes, until tender and wilted. Remove to a colander, run cold water over it, and drain completely.

2. Beat the eggs lightly in a medium-sized bowl and season with salt and pepper. Oil a 12-inch omelet pan and heat the pan for 45 seconds over medium heat. Pour in the eggs and quickly spread the asparagus evenly over them. Sprinkle with grated cheese. Reduce the heat to low and cook the frittata for 12 to 15 minutes, until the eggs are set but not browned.

3. Preheat oven to 450°F. As soon as you remove the omelet pan from the heat, place it in the oven and continue to cook the frittata for another 10 to 15 minutes until set and golden. Slip a spatula around the periphery of the frittata to loosen it and slide it onto a serving plate. Serve hot.

SCRAMBLED EGGS WITH FRESH TOMATO AND PARSLEY

Strapatsatha

1/4 cup olive oil

1 celery rib, trimmed and very finely chopped

4 scallions, trimmed and finely chopped

2 large ripe tomatoes

1 large garlic clove, peeled and finely chopped

1/2 cup finely chopped fresh flat-leaf parsley

4 eggs

Salt and freshly ground black pepper to taste

1. Heat the olive oil in a large skillet and sauté the celery and scallions over medium-low heat until wilted, about 10 minutes.

2. Meanwhile, take one tomato at a time and trim off the base. Hold the tomato from its stem end and grate it on a wide-toothed cheese grater into a bowl. (The skin will tear and the pulp will end up mealy and pulverized in the bowl.) Repeat with remaining tomatoes.

3. Add the garlic to the skillet and stir for about 1 minute. Add the tomatoes and cook over medium heat until most of their liquid has evaporated, 7 to 10 minutes. Add the parsley and stir. Crack the eggs into a bowl, beat slightly, season with salt and pepper, and add them to the skillet. Mix them immediately with a fork to scramble, and cook them to desired consistency. This dish shouldn't be runny but it should be juicy and moist. Adjust seasoning to taste and serve immediately.

Yield: 4 to 6 servings

CONVERSION TABLES

TEMPERATURES

	FAHRENHEIT	CENTIGRADE
Water freezes	32°F	0°C
Water boils	212°F	100°C
Very low oven	250°–275°F	121°–133°C
Low	300°–325°F	149°–163°C
Moderate	350°–375°F	177°–190°C
Hot	400°–425°F	204°–218°C
Very hot	450°–475°F	232°–246°C
Extremely hot	500°–525°F	260°–274°C

To convert Farenheit to Centigrade, subtract 32, multiply by 5, and divide by 9. To convert Centigrade to Farenheit, multiply by 9, divide by 5, and add 32.

DRY MEASURES

1 ounce = 28.35 grams = 16 drams (a measure still used in Greece)

1 pound = 16 ounces = 454 grams

1 gram = .565 dram = .032 ounce = .002 pound = .001 kilo

1 kilo = .000032 ounce = 2.2 pounds = 1000 grams

LIQUID MEASURES

1 teaspoon = 5 milliliters

1 tablespoon = 3 teaspoons = 15 milliliters

1 fluid ounce = 6 teaspoons = 2 tablespoons = 29.56 milliliters = .030 liter

1 cup = 16 tablespoons = 8 fluid ounces = 236 milliliters = .236 liter

1 U.S. pint = 2 cups = 473 milliliters = .473 liter

1 quart = 32 ounces = 4 cups = 946 milliliters = .946 liter

1 liter = 2.113 cups = 1.057 quarts = .264 gallon = 1000 milliliters

Water: 1 cup = 115 grams, 1 pound = 2 cups

LINEAR MEASURES

1 centimeter = .394 inch

1 inch = 2.54 centimeters

1 meter = 39.37 inches

MAIL-ORDER SOURCES

For an enormous variety of Greek products, including herbs, bulgur wheat, cheeses, olives, olive oil, honey, and more:

Krinos Foods, Inc.
47-00 Northern Blvd.
Long Island City, NY 11102

Tel: 718-729-9000
For herbs, olive oil, good vinegars, great beans, and more:

Dean and Deluca
560 Broadway
New York, NY 10012
Tel: 800-221-7714
Tel: 212-431-1691

For nuts, spices, and more:

Kalustyan
123 Lexington Ave.
New York, NY 10016
Tel: 212-685-3416

For Greek-style sheep's milk yogurt:

Hollow Road Farms
Stuyvesant, NY 12173
Tel: 518-758-7214

For wild greens (from seed):

Johnny's Selected Seeds
Foss Hill Road
Albion, ME 04910-9731
Tel: 207-437-4301

Cook's Garden
P.O. Box 535
Londonderry, VT 05148
Tel: 802-824-3400

Other Greek food importers:

Peloponnese
6500 Hollis Street
Ste #10
Emeryville, CA 94608
Tel: 510-547-7356

Titan Foods
25-56 31st Street
Astoria, NY 11102
Tel: 718-626-7771

BIBLIOGRAPHY

Alexiadou, Vefa. *Greek Cuisine*. Thessaloniki: Alexiadou, 1989.

Aligizakis, Manolis. *The Processing and Preservation of Table Olives* (in Greek), Athens: Aligizakis, 1982.

Balatsouras, Yiorgios. *The Table Olive* (in Greek), Athens: Balatsouras, 1992.

Bozi, Soula. *Politiki Kouzina* (in Greek), Athens: Ekdoseis Asterismos, 1994.

Chaitow, Alkmini. *Greek Vegetarian Cooking*, Rochester, Vermont: Healing Art Press, 1989.

Conistis, Peter. Greek Cuisine, *The New Classics*, Berkeley, Cal.: Ten Speed Press, 1994.

Dagher, Shawky M., Ed., *Traditional Foods of the Near East*, Rome: Food and Agriculture Organization of the United Nations, 1991.

Diamanti, Stefanos. *The Mushrooms of Greece* (in Greek), Athens: Ekdoseis Ion, 1992.

Dosithea, Archimandriti. *Opsopoion Magganeiai Ygoun Kaloghriki Mageiriki*, Evritania, Greece: Ieras Monis Tatarnis, 1992.

Filoproodou Omilou Kampou. *Traditional Recipes from Chios* (in Greek), Chios, Greece: 1992.

Frangaki, Evangellia. *Symbolism of Common Greek Plants* (in Greek), Athens: Frangaki, 1969.

Fytraki (Pub). *The Traditional Recipes of Greece* (in Greek), six volumes, Athens: Fytrakis, no date.

Heldreich, Theodore. *Dictionary of the Common Names of the Plants of Greece* (in Greek), reprint of a book first published in 1909, Athens: Adelfon Tolidi, 1980.

Jenkins, Nancy Harmon. *The Mediterranean Diet Cookbook*, New York: Bantam Books, 1994.

Kardoulis, Alexandros. *Trilingual Dictionary of Food and Drink*, Athens: Kardoulis, 1989.

Keltemidis, Dimitris. *The Colloquial Names of Mushrooms in Greece* (in Greek), Athens: Ekdoseis Psihalou, 1986.

————— *Mushrooms of the Mountains and of the Fields* (in Greek), Athens: Ekdoseis Psihalou, 1990.

Kochilas, Diane. *The Food and Wine of Greece,* New York: St. Martin's Press, 1990.

————— "The Glorious Cheeses that are Greek," *New York Times,* October 2, 1991.

Kokkinou, M.D. and Kofina, G.S. *Sarakostiana,* Athens: Ekdoseis Akritas, 1992.

Koutsa, Simeon. *The Fast* (in Greek), Athens: Apostoliki Diakonia, 1991.

Kowalchik, Claire and Hylton, William H., ed. *Rodale's Illustrated Encyclopedia of Herbs,* Emmaus, Penn.: Rodale Press, 1987.

Leschi Gynaikon Karditsas. *Traditional Pies of Karditsa* (in Greek), Karditsa, Greece: 1993.

Louis, Diana Farr and Marinos, June. *Prospero's Kitchen: Mediterranean Cooking of the Ionian Islands,* New York: M. Evans and Company, 1995.

Lyceum of Kallimasia. *Chios Traditional Recipes* (in Greek), Chios, Greece: 1994.

Magoulas, Mihali. *Ithacan Cuisine* (in Greek), self-published, Athens: 1994.

Mallos, Tess. *Greek Cookbook,* Sydney: Lansdowne Press, 1986

Mantanari, Massimo. *The Culture of Food,* Oxford, UK: Blackwell Publishers, 1994.

Mantzaridou, Kaiti. *Lenten Foods and Sweets* (in Greek), Thessaloniki: Ekdoseis P. Pournara, 1994.

Perseli, Anna Emm. *The Cuisine of Kassos* (in Greek), Athens: Perseli, 1994.

Petropoulos, Ilias. *The National Bean Soup and the Omelet* (in Greek), Athens: Nefeli Press, 1993.

Phillips, Roger. *Mushrooms and Other Fungi of Great Britain and Europe,* London: Pan Books, 1981.

Politis, Mihalis, *Olive Cultivation in Corfu* (in Greek), Corfu: Politis, 1982.

Psillakis, Maria and Nikos. *The Traditional Cuisine of Crete* (in Greek), Herakleion, Crete: Karmanor Press, 1995.

Santa Maria, Jack. *Greek Vegetarian Cookery,* Boston: Shambhala Publications, 1984.

Savidi, Lena. *1989 Calendar with 209 Traditional Greek Recipes,* Athens: Ermes Press, 1988.

Sfikas, George. *Medicinal Plants of Greece,* Athens: Efstathiadis Group, 1993.

———— *Trees and Shrubs of Greece,* Athens: Efstathiadis Group, 1993.

Stefopoulos, Andreas. *Traditional Pies of Epiros* (in Greek), Athens: Ekdoseis Pataki, 1991.

Weiss, Gaea and Shandor. *Growing and Using the Healing Herbs,* Avenel, N.J.: Rodale Press, 1992.

Wolfert, Paula. *The Cooking of the Eastern Mediterranean,* New York: HarperCollins Publishers, 1994.

Women's Israelite Society of Volos. *Jewish Holidays and Traditions, a Culinary Guide* (in Greek), Volos, Greece: 1993.

Zouraris, Christos. *The Deipnosophist* (in Greek), Athens: Ikaros Press, 1993.

INDEX